LIBRARY PERSONNEL MANAGEMENT

by Herbert S. White

Knowledge Industry Publications, Inc.
White Plains, NY and London

Professional Librarian Series

Library Personnel Management

Library of Congress Cataloging in Publication Data

White, Herbert S.
  Library Personnel Management

  (The Professional librarian)
  Bibliography: p.
  Includes index.
  1. Library personnel management. 2. Information services—Personnel management. I. Title. II. Series.
  Z682.W65   1985   023'.9   84-26146
  ISBN 0-86729-136-2
  ISBN 0-86729-135-4 (pbk.)

Printed in the United States of America

Copyright © 1985 by Knowledge Industry Publications, Inc., 701 Westchester Ave., White Plains, NY 10604. Not to be reproduced in any form whatever without written permission from the publisher.

10   9   8   7   6   5   4   3   2

Table of Contents

Preface v

1. Basic Concepts in Personnel Management 1
2. Staff Functions in the Library Organizational Structure 23
3. Reconciling Organizational and Individual
   Objectives 39
4. Adapting to Changes in Technology 57
5. Leadership, Supervision and the Decision Process 71
6. Approaches to Decision Making 83
7. Employee Recruitment and Selection 97
8. Career Development, Training and
   Continuing Education 111
9. Job Design and Employee Evaluation 123
10. Wage and Salary Administration 139
11. Communication Today and Beyond 149
12. Present and Future Issues for Library Managers 161

Personnel Problem Exercises 171

Selected Bibliography 197

Index 211

About the Author 214

Dedicated to the memory of Mortimer Taube.

He taught me many things,

but most specifically

that managers must have courage.

Preface

The impetus for writing this book came from a variety of sources. For over twenty-five years I served as a manager of libraries, information centers and information corporations in both the public and private sectors. These organizations have ranged from staffs of two to staffs of 300 and more. For the last nine years I have taught a course in personnel management at Indiana University to students ranging from 22-year-olds in the masters program, with no organizational work experience, to senior administrators returning to the campus for a doctorate degree. Throughout much of this time I have also consulted for corporations and professional societies on various aspects of library administration, development and evaluation, and have presented numerous seminars and workshops on such topics as management communication, delegation, supervisory techniques and performance evaluation.

These experiences have confirmed for me the observations that librarians need to know a great deal about the techniques of personnel administration, but that in fact they know very little. In part, this results from a conscious choice made by individuals who seek to avoid interpersonal communications and difficult decisions through refuge in librarianship, often aided and abetted by guidance counselors who are themselves misguided. It is a disastrous mistake. There are few professions as dependent on successful interpersonal communication and persuasion as ours. As practicing librarians know well, ours is not a book- or periodical-based profession; these are only the tools of the trade. Librarianship is a people profession, and we are only as successful as our ability to interact with others makes us. Most librarians carry at least supervisory if not managerial responsibilities from the first position following graduation. This responsibility may extend "only" to clerks or to students, but much if not most of the success or failure of the library and of these junior professionals will depend on the librarian's ability to persuade or motivate others. In the harshest terms in which this sometimes occurs, it also depends on getting others to do what they are supposed to do.

Many librarians do not easily adapt to the role of managers. By educational preparation many are humanists; by preference most are not driven by a hunger for power and financial success. They would prefer to believe in the innate goodness of all others, and to be guided by the premise that individuals with good intentions will reach common objectives and work cooperatively to achieve these. Techniques are really not required, only good will. This is a comfortable belief, and one that blends well with the development of socio-managerial theories of the 1960s. Behavioral scientists, reflecting the particular societal beliefs of that era, argued that we could move from the original concept of using threats to secure worker compliance, and the later argument that economic stimuli worked better, to the utopian ideal of workers and managers embracing common objectives, with the delineation between classes ultimately blurred or totally eliminated.

These behavioral scientists are not wrong. Much of what they propose has merit, but their arguments are as simplistic as those of the theorists who preceded them. As these shortcomings are perceived in the harsh reality of the workplace, they are rapidly followed by new theories. The success of the Japanese in producing cars of higher quality at lower cost has led to much soul searching and, among other results, to the promulgation of "Theory Z." As this book is being written, there are undoubtedly newly evolving approaches to finding "THE SOLUTION" in typewriters and word processors in Schools of Business and Departments of Sociology throughout the world.

It is precisely this continuing environment of contradiction and confusion which prompted the writing of this book. Operating managers, and most particularly managers in libraries and information centers, do not need more books and articles that describe the latest fad, and that guarantee to improve communication, reduce absenteeism, and enhance work quality and work quantity. Some of these approaches work some of the time, some with some individuals. In a rephrasing of the Abraham Lincoln statement, none of them work for all the people all of the time. This is true because people are different, and because they have different value systems and different expectations. Some want to achieve promotion, participate in organizational decisions, and have interesting and challenging jobs. Some who can be just as useful and satisfactory want none of these things, and the library manager had better be able to tell which is which.

There are generalizations which do apply to personnel management, but they are largely the generalizations which apply to all interpersonal behavior. They do not include such simplistic labels as unilateral decisions, assignment, delegation, consultation, participation and abdication to describe various management styles. In all probability, a case can be made for all of these styles in certain situations; without doubt, no successful case can be made for any of these styles in all situations.

The purpose of this book is to permit library managers, would-be library managers and library school students to develop the assessment tools and judgments to allow them to evaluate each situation and each individual independently, as they deserve to be evaluated. The ability to treat each subordinate as an individual must not obviate the need for predictability and consistency nor the responsibility for effectively managing resources, including people, to accomplish identified organizational objectives. It is the ability to perform all of these sometimes contradictory tasks that makes management difficult and that also makes it worthwhile.

Despite their preconceptions and aversions, librarians can be good managers. Most of them bring to their work both the intelligence and analytical judgments necessary to good management. In any case, since they are going to have to be managers, they might as well be good ones. If they avoid the opportunity and responsibility, those chosen in their stead might be worse. Managers can do their jobs badly for a variety of reasons, and for every administrator who commits the sin of functioning autocratically and making decisions willfully and haphazardly, there are at least as many who are paralyzed by the decision process and who will not decide anything at all. In my experience, library managers fall into the second category far more frequently than the first. What is perceived as an autocratic style is often a noncommunicative style, and the reason for the lack of communication is not only the failure to understand its importance but also the fact that vacillating managers have nothing to communicate.

For those, and there are many in our profession, who fear the responsibility of decision making, the suggestion that managers should be more democratic has been a godsend. The establishment of a profusion of committees in the name of democracy can serve to delay the reaching of decisions even further, and can blur responsibility even more. Suggesting to decision-avoidance managers that they should encourage more participation is the same as handing an alcoholic a glass of whiskey. The tactic does not work either for the success of the library or for the morale of its staff, because individuals learn quickly when their time is being wasted on sham participation, and when they are asked questions to no particular purpose. This makes them more resentful than when they were not asked at all. It helps neither morale nor the quality of decisions when librarians are dragged into meetings they consider pointless and an intrusion on their own work schedule. As this book will stress repeatedly, no two institutions or individuals are alike, and generalizations are therefore very dangerous.

However, if we understand anything at all about what workers want, it is some control over their own specific work environment and job arrangement. In addition, they want the right to provide input to a management decision if they have an opinion to express, with assurance that their suggestions will be considered and evaluated. What is lacking in most cases is not a sharing of power, it is a sharing of common objectives and purposes, and a sharing of how and why decisions were made and what their impact will be. The missing ingredient in most organizations, and certainly in most libraries, is communication. Communication is not expensive to provide, but the failure to provide it can be very expensive.

This book does not attempt to repeat in depth the literature of personnel administration, because it is generally and easily available. Volumes have been devoted to such specific and narrow topics as interviewing, hiring, training, delegating, promoting and firing. The periodical literature is even more detailed and specific, although the reader is warned that much of it consists of slogans and cheerleading. It is because of this wealth of easily accessible literature that I have not placed suggested further readings at the end of each chapter. A relatively brief and very selective bibliography lists additional works in the general management literature, as well as writings directly oriented to personnel management in libraries. In the first instance, there is far too much written to permit a semblance of coping; in the second, there is little which does not already represent conclusions looking for a justification.

There are three monographs that I have found very useful and which I recommend to those who wish to study these issues in greater depth. The first of these is Dale S. Beach's *Personnel, The Management of People at Work.* This book, currently in its fourth edition (1980), is published by Macmillan. As a general management textbook it is thorough, and it places less emphasis than most such works on the production and marketing supervisory issues so inappropriate for library study. Some have found its terminology to be sexist, but that is a characteristic of much of the management literature, particularly older writings. The second work is Loren B. Belker's *The First-Time Manager,* published by the American Management Association in 1978. This witty and wise little book can probably be read at one easy sitting, and then reused for specific comments and suggestions. In the library field I am very impressed by Murray S. Martin's *Issues in Personnel Management in Academic Libraries* (JAI Press, 1981). Despite the narrow focus of its title, this work presents valuable insights for any library administrator, as well as a strong bibliography of additional readings.

It is my hope that my own book can be read by library managers and can then wait on their office shelves to be consulted again as needed. This is not a book on "how to manage," because specific and individual issues defy pre-solution. It is a book which enables the reader to identify and analyze personnel management problems and, hopefully, one which will contribute to the manager's ability to arrive at the correct solutions to specific problematic situations as they arise. Any experienced manager knows that they will indeed arise in the most unexpected time and place.

Personnel problem exercises are an effective technique for coming to grips with management issues, and a small number are presented at the end of the book. Individuals who plan to use this as a textbook will want to supplement them with other problem exercises or case studies which are increasingly available in the library literature, or they may prefer to develop their own to illustrate a specific point or concern, as I continue to do in teaching my courses.

I wish to express my appreciation to the thousands of individuals whom I have encountered in a variety of management situations who have unknowingly and unwittingly contributed to this book. However, a number of individuals must be specifically thanked. These include my wife Virginia, who read every word of this manuscript and turned my naturally complex sentences into simpler ones. Emily Gallup Fayen provided suggestions and reference materials for the chapter dealing with adaptation to changes in technology. Two secretaries in the Indiana University School of Library and Information Science, Martha Geter and Sheri Allen, typed the manuscript from notes not always easy to decipher. To all of these individuals I am grateful.

Herbert S. White
February 1985

1

Basic Concepts in Personnel Management

Before one can examine and analyze management precepts and practices, specifically in the library setting, it is first necessary to define what we mean by a "manager." For purposes of the present work, a manager is any individual entrusted with control over the use of resources—both in personnel and material.

The recognition that the management of subordinates is the best way to improve the performance of any organization forms the basis for the development of personnel administration theories and concepts. This awareness is a comparatively recent phenomenon, with virtually all realizations and resulting reforms occurring in the 20th century, most of it following World War II. Recent as such concepts are in personnel management literature, they are even newer when applied to librarianship.

Nevertheless, the need for effective personnel management in libraries should be clear. Libraries have long been labor-intensive organizations. In studies undertaken for the National Science Foundation, covering the years 1968 to 1978, I consistently found that far more than half of the library budget, in any type of library, was spent on salaries. For academic and special libraries the percentage ranged from 60% to close to 70%. For public libraries with branches and long hours of opening, the figure sometimes surpassed 80%. It can therefore be argued that, despite the fascination of users with the size and sometimes specific content of the collection, a library is only as good as its staff. Its allocation of resources is only as effective as the way in which it uses its personnel.

The same studies indicated that as library budgets began to tighten in the late 1970s and early 1980s, the percentage of total budget spent for salaries tended to increase even further. This occurred because most organizations, be they universities, municipal governments or private corporations, often tended to emphasize salary increases over other alternatives for spending scarce resources, since such actions earn greater visibility and credit, and forestall confrontation and problems with subordinates. Other needs are frequently postponed, sometimes indefinitely.

In some sectors of the economy this is not considered a problem. As labor costs rise, these increases are simply passed along to the end consumer without much concern. At least that has been a long-standing industrial practice in many business settings.

Libraries are generally perceived, and most particularly in academia, as collections of materials. When it appears that salaries of library personnel are getting in the way of acquiring books and journals, problems rapidly ensue. Usually these result in pressures that the library grant smaller salary increases than those awarded in other academic units, that it decrease the library staff to avoid the continuing transfer of scarce resources into the salary budget, or that it do both of these. Libraries have never been particularly successful in clarifying objectives or priorities, in identifying the personnel resources required to carry out approved programs, or in forcing those in administrative levels higher than the library to take responsibility for freezing or reducing the library budget. Ever-increasing pressures on library staff to accomplish more, without any understanding of how this is to be achieved, ensue. This is a phenomenon which underlies much of personnel management complexity for libraries, and it will be addressed in far greater detail later in this book.

In addition to all of these severe problems, libraries have also, at least until a short while ago, had little relief from internal pressures to award salary increases of greater percentage than the total budget growth, and to increase staffing in direct relationship to increased quantities of workload. As William Baumol, Fritz Machlup and other economists have noted, librarians have until recently seen few alternatives to coupling linear workload increases with linear staffing increases.

INCREASING EFFICIENCY: PROBLEMS AND GOALS

Laborsaving devices have permitted substantial wage growth in various manufacturing industries, because they either decreased the need for workers or increased the productivity of the individual worker. For example, such devices enabled American agriculture to produce more and more farm products with fewer and fewer people. Laborsaving equipment has simply not been available to United States librarians. Nor has there been any impetus to find such resources, since proponents of production efficiency did not perceive libraries as fruitful targets for their efforts. Librarians, primarily trained as humanists, and without either management education or management values, would have made them feel unwelcome in any case. Still, the belated application of automation to libraries offers potential for productivity increases and personnel reductions. These developments can cause a great deal of animosity and unrest, reactions certainly not new to American industry but very new to libraries. Ours remains a people-oriented profession.

While innovations that allow people to work more efficiently or at more interesting tasks are usually welcome, economic solutions that lead to staff cuts are not. Approaches that make libraries more effective, but at a greater overall cost, are not as welcome as they might be in manufacturing; improving the quality of library service is considered desirable but not as obviously productive as increasing the gross national product.

Library managers will most certainly be confronted with the need to accomplish more with a staff that does not increase in size. One can only hope that they will not be faced with demands for massive reductions in library staffing. Simply asking people to work harder, to catalog twice as many books, or answer twice as many reference questions, will not work. Technology may help, but its introduction brings problems of its own. There is the clearly predictable phenomenon of increasing needs, expectations and complexity, tied to flat budget and staffing projections, and the aversion of almost all workers to the suggestion that they simply must do more. Inevitably, we turn to people as our primary resource and as our best hope for the future. The way to make libraries more effective is to make people more effective. Without that, probably nothing else will work.

Librarians As Humanists

At first glance, the problem in libraries is no different from that in the rest of society. All fields are beleaguered by growing absenteeism, lowered productivity, rising alienation, and an unfavorable comparison to accomplishments in Japan and other cultures. And yet there are differences which tend to make things even more difficult for librarians. One of the most important of these differences is that librarians have traditionally been humanists. They have loved ideas and books, and have felt that concepts of measurement, reward and punishment were manipulative machinations which had no place in this profession.

In the early 1970s, for the first time, library managers began to hear phrases such as "cost-effectiveness," "management by objectives," "added value" and "zero base budgeting." The premise of libraries as part of the educational experience began to come under scrutiny. This process was accelerated by economic retrenchment and the impact of earlier declines in the birth rate. The initial reaction of librarians was predictably one of hurt and confusion, together with cries of "foul play."

In 1978, in a keynote address to the Canadian Library Association, later published in the October 1978 issue of that society's journal, I commented on this phenomenon:

> Librarians are most often humanists, rarely scientists or engineers. They are drawn into the field because of their love of books, their love of knowledge and their idealistic desire to contribute to the making of a better society.... Their approach to management is at best wary, at worst openly hostile. Management, they instinctively feel, is a conspiracy to keep people from doing what they want to do and make them do what some one else wants. It is repressive, it is devious, it is undemocratic. People should be allowed to make their own decisions and do what they want to do, because we all have the interests of the library and of society at heart.... The suggestion made to circumvent the need to justify and explain is that libraries are self-evidently good. If things are self-evident, they don't need to be explained or justified. This has been the precise tactic in support of library services throughout the 19th century and this part of the 20th century. We hold this truth to be self-evident: that library service is good, that more library service is better, and that most library service is best....

The simple justification of the library as self-evidently good no longer works, if it ever did. Perhaps there are too many philistines in high places, but more likely it is because there are too many self-evidently good services in society for us to support each at the level of desired support.

An earlier indication of the trauma being experienced by library administrators can be found in an article by Arthur McAnally and Robert Downs in the March 1973 issue of *College and Research Libraries.* Surveying the 78 largest academic libraries in the United States, they found that half had changed directors in the last three years, four of them twice. Retirements accounted for only a small percentage of the changes. Similar, even if not quite as dramatic, statistics were reported for smaller libraries.

Setting Attainable Goals

Unrealistic expectations of library users undoubtedly played a role in creating these pressures, but an even more significant reason for the development of these major problems is the lack of discipline and organization of the library staff. An unwillingness to establish priorities and objectives follows naturally enough from the argument that everything we do is "self-evidently good" and therefore does not need to be justified. Libraries are goal-oriented, but some goals are idealistic statements which cannot be used for planning and evaluation. The more specific criteria of objectives, programs and strategies have been noticeably absent in libraries. The goal orientation has been toward acquisition and growth of the collection, and the expansion of services without limits. Limitless objectives are feasible only when resources are limitless. The unwillingness of administrators, users and librarians to apply limits and make hard choices in the face of constant or declining resources has put unbearable pressures on the staff to accomplish more and more with less and less.

People often do not mind working hard if they can achieve some finite objectives. They are willing to play the game, but they would like a chance to win. In the refusal, or at least reluctance, to deal with the reality of finite staffs and resources, libraries can create untenable pressures. Some of these result from an unwillingness to accept the librarian's overall role and standing. In the academic community, librarians have striven for faculty status. This is not a bad aspiration, when it is recognized that faculty members enjoy not only greater pay but much greater security. However, this desire to emulate faculty has failed to come to grips with the fact that librarians do not work like faculty. They do not spend 10 or 12 hours per week in the classroom, with the rest of the week and the summer free for planning, research and other activities, time for which the faculty member is not accountable.

Librarians work 40-hour or 35-hour shifts, regularly scheduled. They work in hierarchical, bureaucratic organizations not given either to the appropriateness of seeking total staff involvement in decisions arrived at through consensus, or the adequacy of time needed to grope toward such total agreement. When faculty members attend committee meetings, they do so during the time they are not teaching, and enough time is provided for this activity. When librarians attend committee meetings, their work continues to accumulate. It was assigned on the premise that they would be there all of the time. It is therefore not surprising that librarians, drawn to the promises of the "better life" inherent in participation and job enrichment, become more quickly disillusioned when they see few of the benefits and all of the personal hardships.

While the evolution of personnel management techniques in libraries has largely come about as a result of theories and experiments developed to make the industrial working place more effective, as later discussion will show, none of these premises of personnel theory—of a more open environment which leads to greater benefits in higher quality and quantity of work—are successful all of the time. Personnel management, in libraries as elsewhere, is not an exact science dealing with clear alternatives of right and wrong. Many times personnel management deals with the need to make choices among alternatives, none of which is particularly attractive, when it is clear that some action must be taken.

Personnel management is complex because people are complex, and don't always respond as the case study or textbook would indicate. While some employees leap eagerly at opportunities to participate in the decision process and expand job horizons, others would rather continue in the safety of doing what they have always done, without risk or responsibility. They would, of course, like to be rewarded *as though* they were taking risks and experiencing growth.

The Need for Identifiable Limits

All of these problems and concerns are generic to any working environment, and are not particular to libraries. But the problems for libraries may sometimes be increased by those institutions' unique characterisics, some of which have already been mentioned. Libraries have broad goals (such as "to serve the academic community") but few concrete, measurable objectives. Given finite resources, it is at least as important to define what will *not* be done as it is to postulate what can be accomplished. Without this criterion, library workers are playing a game without rules, without scores and without time limits.

There is nothing wrong in involving staff members in the development of rules and playing-field boundaries. Totally autocratic concepts do not work well in any managerial context. However, the rules and boundaries must have some relation to reality, and that reality is most directly expressed in resource support. Libraries that cry poverty but insist that they are wonderful nonetheless create a dichotomy in the eyes of those in ultimate authority. As idealists, librarians find it difficult to reject idealistic if impractical approaches. And yet reject them they must.

As optimists about human nature, librarians prefer to avoid issues of supervision and the giving of instructions. They prefer cooperation and agreement, but fail to understand that, for most of us, cooperation means that "others do things our way." When we agree that we all have the best interests of the library at heart, it does not follow that we all agree what those interests are and how we can best achieve them.

Individuals do not like authoritarianism and regimentation. They do not like to lose continually without even having known the rules. However, it is not necessary to them that they win all the time, either. It is only important to know why they lost, and to be assured that they will have another chance to win, if they play better. If the reader begins to see a similarity between library organization and organized games, that similarity is intentional.

Playing games without rules, or games in which the rules can be changed at will, is very little fun and provides very little satisfaction.

If librarians have even more difficulty with concepts of personnel administration than others, it is perhaps for three reasons:

1) Libraries lack clear direction of what they need to accomplish, in both the long and short term. Their staffs do not know what it takes to win.

2) Librarians are seldom authority-oriented. They do not like rules, in an environment which is both bureaucratic and hierarchical. Neither of these is a pejorative term. Both are simply descriptive.

3) Librarians tend to seek direct and specific answers to complex problems. Perhaps that approach works in cataloging. It does not work in personnel administration.

The Need for Flexibility

Two points must be kept in mind when considering personnel management. The first is that generalizations must be greeted with skepticism. What will work in some settings and with some individuals will not work with others. The "laws" of personnel administration are not like the laws of physics. (As a later heading in this chapter indicates, however, some generalizations are worthwhile.)

Second, personnel administration is an area of constant change. New theories and concepts will evolve, most of them with high-flown promises. Some will fail abysmally, while others will simply be restatements of old truths. Still others may contain a kernel of useful information about people and what motivates them. One of the characteristics which most accurately describes the development of personnel management theories is that of a pendulum. We eventually perceive excesses in many of these theories and, to compensate, we swing in the other direction, creating new and opposite excesses.

In many ways, theories of personnel administration share some of the characteristics of political analysis. New presidents enter office amid a great many hopes and expectations. It is usually only after a period of perhaps 20 years that analysts consider it safe to review the accomplishments and failures dispassionately and objectively. In librarianship also we are unable to evaluate our own progress dispassionately while we have a personal stake in the solution. In addition, some theories lend themselves more readily to the library setting than others, especially because of the personality characteristics particular to library personnel.

The economic theory of motivation developed by Frederick Taylor and his collaborators (which is discussed below in greater detail) contained many truths, but also many oversimplifications. The social theory of motivation that holds that people work better if they are contented also has some validity but much inaccuracy as well. Many managers have come to see the flaws in such concepts as they realize that personnel administration is both tough and individualistic. Others will cling stubbornly to the conclusions that arose from new value systems developed during the 1960s. Any manager must be constantly reminded to attempt to maintain objectivity, or at least to realize those issues for which objectivity is not possible. Without this capacity one is lost.

PERSONNEL MANAGEMENT THEORIES

With this background, it is time to undertake a very brief survey of personnel administration as a general concept. To do so is not for the purpose of making the reader an expert on this subject, but rather so that he or she realizes that we are dealing with an evolving and amorphous concept. Personnel theory changes as "perfect" solutions are sought. These will never be found, and therefore change will be continuous. Hopefully, as we change we improve, but we cannot even be certain of that.

As already noted, personnel management is a recent concern. Until the late 19th century little attention was paid to motivation and incentives. People worked because they had to, and they worked to arbitrary standards set by their supervisors. Under slavery the manager/worker relationship is obvious, but even in the early industrial revolution the supervisor had absolute power to hire and fire, without explanation or justification. If the decision was wrong or unfair, there was not only no appeal, but also no one to make that determination.

Classical Theories

Most library organizational structure is still based on three distinct and yet somewhat overlapping traditional organizational theories. They are scientific management, administrative management and the bureaucratic model. All of these started to be actively developed and implemented at the beginning of the 20th century. Antiquated as some of these concepts now may seem, it should be remembered that all of them represented substantial advances over what had preceded them.

The concept of scientific management was developed by Frederick Taylor and his followers near the turn of the century. Taylor postulated greater productivity and lower costs by removing planning responsibility from the worker and transferring it to a management specialist. Scientific management is based on the premises of the Protestant work ethic and of rational, competitive workers motivated by the promise of economic gain.

The concept of administrative management was championed by individuals such as Henri Fayol, Luther Gulick and Lyndall Urwick. It postulated a division of labor and specialization of function as most efficient, with coordination of these activities to be performed by the manager. It argued for a strict chain of command which was not to be bypassed, with both responsibility and authority clearly delineated for each manager. Authority was seen as emanating from the top downward, and responsibility equaled authority. It was further argued that any one individual could have only one boss. A supervisor's ability to control the work of subordinates was limited to perhaps five or six, and at best only a few more. The reader will recognize many of the characteristics of present-day library administration in this concept, as well as in the one that follows. With few exceptions, library organizations have only recently begun to deviate from these models, although such concepts have been attacked by behavioral scientists for more than 30 years.

The bureaucratic model of organizational behavior was articulated by Max Weber, who saw it as part of an overall view of society, incorporating religion and politics, and based on the premise of an ever more rational and secular society. Weber intensified the administrative management approach to specialization and authority. However, he added a system of rules impersonally administered, without favoritism or nepotism. Employment, assignment and advancement were to be based wholly on qualifications, and satisfactory performance assured job security. It was inevitable that such a concept would be buttressed by the extensive use of records, documents and files.

Criticisms of the Classical Theories

It is important to recognize in the 1980s, when we now regard these theories as impersonal and insensitive to individual aspirations, what a tremendous step forward they represented. In basing qualifications on "what you know" rather than "whom you know," these classical theories have served us reasonably well. While it is appropriate to look at revisions and modifications, it would be a mistake to eliminate these concepts entirely, especially if we have no concrete theories with which to replace them.

In any event, the classical theories have been criticized, in many cases quite appropriately, by a large group of behavioral scientists. This group, whose writing is still very much in vogue today, includes Elton Mayo, Douglas McGregor, Rensis Likert, Frederick Herzberg, Warren Bennis and Chris Argyris. They argued that the classical theories of organizational structure took a mechanistic view of people. This view assumed that individuals were pliant and submissive, and would be satisfied to do what they were told to do as long as monetary motivation was provided. The behavioral scientists argued for more attention to attitudes, morale and group relationship, and stated that instead of shaping people to jobs, we should be shaping jobs to people. They also propounded an optimistic view of the nature of man, insisting that high performance can be better achieved by self-direction and control than by rigid regulation.

Initially developed for hourly or blue-collar workers, the emphasis in these later theories quickly expanded to include white-collar and professional workers, including librarians. Librarians, for their part, have embraced such concepts as participative management, flextime, job enrichment and job rotation with eagerness.

The time for these more progressive theories was propitious. The United States was concurrently entering an era of greater awareness of social responsibility, both by the employer and by the government, which reached its zenith in the Great Society programs of Lyndon Johnson. Laws were developed to emphasize management responsibilities to the worker, and to protect individual job rights. Behavioral scientists told us not only that this was fair and decent, but that it also made economic sense. We should recognize, however, the very shaky basis for this economic justification.

For example, there is no shred of evidence to indicate that the widely held assumption that increased productivity results from greater happiness is true. There is evidence to tie reduced productivity to discontent and uncertainty. Flexible work schedules and job sharing may indeed be societal objectives worth achieving regardless of cost, but to suggest that such virtue brings its own economic rewards would be to ignore evidence for the sake of conclusions.

The concepts proposed by the behavioral scientists have, in turn, been attacked as being soft on workers, tolerating poor performance and ignoring the impacts of technology and economic change. Perhaps most paradoxically, they have been criticized as being manipulative in the attempt to persuade people with ideas rather than with authority and power.

Recognition of Individual Differences

Individuals are too complex to permit themselves to be summed up by simplistic theories. The behavioral scientists who observed heavy absenteeism on Fridays, and from this argued that a four-day work week from Monday to Thursday would reap economic benefits, failed to deal with the reasons for high absenteeism on Friday. Where four-day work weeks were put into practice, the high absenteeism simply shifted to Thursday.

Many factors affect human behavior, and attempts to predict them will never be successful all of the time. Individuals constantly shift and rerank their needs. Librarians, who were initially scornful of unionization because they saw no advantage in such a step, become more interested in the protection which unions afford as they are faced with the potential of layoffs. So-called "give-backs" in economic negotiation are unheard of during periods of high employment. At other times, contract negotiations may concern not the amount of pay increase, but the amount of pay cut.

The assumption that the industrial success enjoyed by the Japanese could be emulated by simply transferring it across the Pacific Ocean is unrealistic and has fortunately been replaced by the realization that many modifications are required, although some benefits can be realized and much can be learned. Americans are not Japanese. They have different outlooks toward work and different attitudes toward supervision.

Without doubt, greater refinements in organizational theory have brought valuable new insights. However, any attempt to implement new concepts without regard to the specific organization is bound to fail. Each library must develop an organizational approach which fits its goals and objectives, its personnel and its environment. Standardized approaches are bound to fail, because fundamentally *how* change is implemented is far more important than *what* change is implemented.

GENERAL RULES FOR PERSONNEL MANAGEMENT

Are there statements that can be made in general about basic qualifications for *any* manager? As the springboard for further detailed discussion, a few such generalizations can be stated.

It is a general perception, as buttressed by countless popular films and television shows, that managers tend to be autocratic, unreasonable, ill-tempered, dictatorial, closed-minded and insistent on making all decisions. That was certainly the correct image of the 19th century foreman and perhaps even of the 20th century non-union shop supervisor. There are undoubtedly such managers today in various organizations, including libraries. In libraries, however, that is not the main thrust of the problem.

The far greater problem, and certainly the more common one in libraries, is with managers who will not manage at all. These individuals will go to almost any lengths to avoid making a decision or avoid taking a risk. They may or may not be pleasant individuals. Incompetents are frequently amiable and likable. However, managers who refuse to manage are disastrous because they create voids and uncertainties. We know that the individual psyche can deal with bad news much more readily than with uncertainty. This factor will receive considerably greater attention later in this book.

Present-day managers, particularly in libraries, are not and cannot be the all-powerful autocrats managers are assumed to be. Their ability to hire and fire is organizationally and legally constrained, and quite properly so. The freedom to award salary increases, promotions and work assignments is also subject to many rules. The authority of the present-day manager is therefore limited, but much authority remains. Subordinates (and the term is used intentionally as a clearer alternative to "colleagues" in a hierarchical environment) may have their own ideas about decision involvement and power-sharing. Even the most radical worker accepts the fact that in a hierarchical organization authority and responsibility are not equally distributed. Employees expect managers to make decisions. They want consistent decisions, the rationale for which will be explained. What subordinates frequently encounter instead is unpredictability—a manager who is sometimes impetuous, sometimes lethargic, sometimes pleasant, sometimes harsh. They perceive an individual who insists on making insignificant decisions but refuses to make important ones, and who gives at least the appearance of favoritism. This fosters an atmosphere of uncertainty, and uncertainty and indecision undermine the resolve and morale of an organization far more than consistent and predictable autocracy, unpleasant and inefficient as such traits may be.

The remainder of this chapter describes some of the characteristics that define any successful manager and certainly a successful manager of personnel in libraries.

Fairness

Managers must be perceived as fair. It was said of Vince Lombardi, coach of the Green Bay Packers football team, that he treated all of his players equally by treating them all like dogs. Lombardi was a successful coach, but is not necessarily held out as a role model for library managers. Nevertheless, the concept of fairness—of displaying no favoritism to anyone—is even more important than the question of whether managers are harsh or permissive.

Consistency and Flexibility

Managers must be both consistent and flexible. Subordinates learn to adapt to consistency and develop a mechanism for dealing with it. They cannot deal with uncertainty. Such questions anxiously posed to a secretary as, "What sort of mood is the boss in? Is this a good day to talk to him (her)?" reveal a poor manager inside the office.

At the same time, managers must also be flexible. The need to keep consistency and flexibility in balance creates one of the greatest difficulties for the manager. Problems must be viewed in the light of organizational objectives and individual fairness. A retreat to the presumed safety of quoting company policies and procedures is of no value if in a particular instance the policies—which are inevitably phrased to deal with the general and not the specific—do not produce an appropriate or fair result. Policies and procedures do not solve problems; people do. One of the legitimate complaints about policy questions resolved through computer printout is that computer programs resolve such issues consistently but unreasonably. Individual managers are expected to do better. If not, they give rise to the suggestion that perhaps they could be replaced by a computer terminal, at a great saving of money which could then be redistributed to the rest of the staff.

Ability to Grasp New Ideas

Managers must be able to grasp new ideas and concepts. Without this ability, they will stifle all initiative and interest among their subordinates. Not all change is beneficial, but all growth and progress come from change. Some subordinates seek change (particularly when it provides them more opportunity or authority). Others fear any alteration. Both extremes must be dealt with and overcome. However, the second problem is worse than the first. A library that fails to change at all will automatically become worse. As the surrounding environment becomes inevitably more dynamic, the library will suffer by comparison.

Open-mindedness

Managers must be open-minded to the ideas of others. The manager who thinks he or she knows everything better than members of the staff is a fool, and little of redeeming value can be said about such a person. The encouragement of ideas from subordinates not only arouses their participation and interest, it also may generate some good and useful ideas. Not all the suggestions will be useful or even carefully thought out. Only a small percentage may be worthwhile. However, the need to reject some suggestions (as long as the reasons for the rejections are thought out and explained) is far preferable to getting no suggestions at all. A manager who gets no suggestions must take stock. Either this is a staff totally lacking in ambition and imagination, or the impression has been created (perhaps unwittingly) that the presentation of new ideas is unwelcome and dangerous.

Ambition

Managers must be ambitious and forward-looking. Nowhere is this injunction more important than in a library, where it is frequently easy to change nothing without alarming either library patrons or higher level administrators. Individuals work best to meet goals they accept as meaningful, and that they have a realistic opportunity to achieve. An organization that offers its employees only a continuation of routine and a hope for survival offers little incentive for trying harder. The need for ambition and forward planning is most critical during times of financial stringency. During times of affluence—and there may still be some librarians who remember these times—ambitions and new targets usually present themselves.

Ability to Communicate

Good managers must know how to communicate. Communication is a two-way process, and it requires a receiver as well as a transmitter. Subordinates expect communication downward but, too frequently, under the excuse of time pressures, that communication is limited to orders or instructions, without explanation or interpretation. People are more difficult to manage than machines because people want to know *why*. That one-word question emerges in very early childhood; we never stop asking it. It is not essential that the answer to "Why?" yield a response with which the questioner agrees—although that is obviously ideal. It is important that the subordinate be satisfied in the knowledge that the decision was not capricious, that there indeed is a reason and that management knows what it is.

Communication also requires a willingness to listen to ideas, suggestions and comments. Not all subordinates will want to take advantage of this opportunity, and none should be forced to do so. This is not a classroom in which everyone must volunteer or be penalized. However, those individuals who are willing to contribute ideas and reactions should always feel free to do so. They should not feel they are being patronized or that there is risk if their idea differs from their manager's preconceptions. Where either of these situations exists, individuals are quick to grasp and adapt to them. Such pseudo-communication, quickly identified as hypocritical, is far worse than no communication at all. One of the dangers of the concept of "participative management" is that it may encourage individuals to risk stating their own points of view in situations in which this is neither expected nor welcomed. Persons thus burned will quickly adapt, and they will resent having been taken advantage of. (The concept of participative management will be discussed in detail in Chapter 6.)

Another aspect of communications skills is the ability to convey bad news and criticism. This is as important as the distribution of praise and good news, which does not normally pose a problem. Managers are more than happy to share such good communications with members of their staffs. However, not all outside decisions with regard to budgets, staffing, promotions and salary increases are pleasant. Individuals recognize this, and recognize the inevitability of such communications at times. Bad news must be communicated when it exists, and this must be done quickly, simply and sympathetically. The chances are good that subordinates have heard the evil tidings already through the grapevine. It is not unlikely that their perception is even more drastic than reality, because rumor tends to exaggerate in the search for a better story.

Similarly, it is part of the responsibility of the supervisor to criticize where criticism is warranted. He or she must do this directly and specifically, and with an emphasis on future change rather than on past deficiencies. Most employees do not particularly enjoy criticism; few individuals do. However, a whole array of personnel surveys indicate that they can accept it if it concentrates on improvement rather than on vindictive punishment. They particularly and quite rightfully insist on being confronted with the supervisor's criticism if actions with regard to promotions, salary increases and perhaps even termination are going to be based on that supervisory perception of performance.

Leadership

Leadership will exist and develop in any organization, but it is far preferable if the real leader is also the individual actually in charge. Where managers do not exercise leadership, leadership patterns will evolve from within the group. The effectiveness of this development will depend on whether the group-leader's objectives agree with those of the administration. There is an instinctive expectation or desire from all but the most hard-core anarchists that those assigned higher posts with greater authority and reward will also lead. In more rigidly bureaucratic structures, such as the Japanese industrial organization, that expectation becomes an insistence, because if managers will not lead, nobody else will. In the United States an alternate leader will probably evolve, but the direction of that leadership may produce risk. Leadership qualities, which will be discussed in greater detail in Chapter 5, are probably more inherent than acquired. It is not surprising that the United States Army spends considerable effort in identifying potential noncommissioned officers, and that foremen are frequently chosen from among the group of former union shop stewards.

One of the inherent reasons why leadership among managers is not as prevalent as it ought to be, particularly in libraries, is because we tend to select our managers with other criteria in mind. These include seniority, strong performance in a technical assignment, and a pleasant and affable disposition. Paradoxically, this last factor may be—although certainly not automatically—a negative indicator. Leaders are not automatically disputatious, but they must be prepared to be when disputation is appropriate and warranted.

Idealism Tempered with Pragmatism

Successful managers must represent a blend of idealism and pragmatism. Lofty goals which inspire others are important, but they must be tempered with objectives that are achievable, and with plans and strategies designed to achieve them. Managers must recognize that perfect solutions are rare, and optimal resources nonexistent. Managers must therefore always deal in achieving not only what should be achieved, but also in what can or cannot be achieved, even by dint of hard effort.

Library employees are members of a team, and all team members like to win at least some of the time. If they perceive that the rules of the game have been stacked against every possible chance of success, either by the expression of idealistic goals as objectives or by the acceptance of unreasonable premises for the library organization, their morale will quickly turn to cynicism and disenchantment. If they perceive that regardless of their efforts the results will be exactly the same, they will react accordingly.

Ability to Set Priorities

Managers must be able to differentiate between what is important and what is trivial. They must expend their limited resources of time and energy on those activities which are important enough to warrant their attention. This is not easy, because it requires a considerable amount of self-discipline. In many cases, the tasks that are too trivial to warrant the manager's attention or that can be as effectively performed by others are also the most interesting. The problem is complicated in situations in which a manager supervises a group in which he or she had worked very effectively. It is understandable that such a manager would want to continue to operate at the earlier level of decision making, particularly because he or she is probably able to make such decisions well, perhaps better than those now charged with the responsibility of making lower-level decisions.

Sometimes an insistence on operating at a level of detail or trivia is based on the understandable desire to function in an environment in which we feel safe and comfortable. Sometimes it is based on a genuine desire to be helpful to individuals who are or appear to be struggling. Whatever the reason, the manager's intrusion is inappropriate.

Ability to Delegate

Managers must also be able to delegate. Much has been written on this topic in the general management literature, and this book will explore some of these precepts in greater detail as they pertain to libraries. For now it will suffice to state that the need for delegation is generally accepted as a truism, but that in practice it works badly if at all, either because individuals fail to delegate or because they delegate improperly. There are many reasons for a failure to delegate. Most of them are rationalizations. In many instances preconceptions about what cannot be delegated because subordinates are unable, unprepared or unwilling to accept such assignments lead to actions that turn these assumptions into self-fulfilling prophecies.

Courage

Last, and probably most important among the characteristics which identify the successful manager, is courage. Managers must be prepared to fight for what their libraries deserve in the allocation of scarce resources. Much has been written on this subject because the crucial needs of libraries are not as obvious and easily demonstrated as those of police departments or fire protection agencies, or even elementary education.

Courage is also particularly required in the personnel management setting in making the tough and perhaps unpopular decisions referred to earlier, and most specifically in fighting for subordinates when they are in the right. This quality can emerge in many forms. It can include doing battle against a large and bureaucratic organization which has decided that "according to policy" an inequity may be unfortunate but also "unavoidable," which means that it is too much trouble to correct. It can also include protection against unfair harrassment from library users, a situation not as uncommon as might be assumed in either an academic or special library setting. Some professors and corporate administrators may consider librarians as unimportant and having neither rights nor feelings. Patrons are even more likely to include library clerks in that category, and the manager's responsibility to them is no less than that due his professional employees.

There are some very fundamental issues at stake. If you expect loyalty, you must give loyalty in return. You will not succeed all of the time, but your subordinates know that and cannot fault you for it. What is important is that you try. Raising such issues may make you unpopular with your own management. It is even more likely to displease such service organizations as the personnel and accounting departments which sometimes think the organization's purpose is to implement their procedure, and forget that the purpose of procedures is to facilitate the work of the organization. Thomas Galvin, Dean of the University of Pittsburgh's School of Library and Information Science, has put this point well and succinctly: "Management is a Contact Sport."

In general, however, it can be stated that people who work in libraries share the hopes, fears, ambitions, frustrations, preconceptions and reactions of people in the work force anywhere. Libraries have a mix of the motivated and dedicated and of the selfish and scheming. Perhaps the percentages differ, but we do not really even know that. We do know that anyone who thinks that individuals who work in libraries can be treated without sensitivity and regard because, after all, they are "dedicated," is building his or her personnel policy on a very shaky base.

2

Staff Functions in the Library Organizational Structure

This chapter will undoubtedly be the one most heavily laden with personnel management theory, and the writer therefore approaches it with some hesitation and caution. This book is not intended as a treatise on management theory but rather as a tool to help with the practical problems of personnel management in the library. Nevertheless, some grounding in theory is necessary.

Many librarians may consider any discussion of organization structure as hypothetical or irrelevant, since most libraries operate with small staffs and only a fraction of these employees are professionals. The careful delineating of organizational relationships becomes something of a useless luxury when the total staff numbers three. When the phone rings, somebody answers it. When a patron walks into the library, that patron normally addresses the first person available and expects at least a willing listener.

It is true that developing an organizational structure to meet the specific needs of a library has never provided, and will never provide, a finite solution if other problems exist. Organizational changes provide no relief from incompetence or irresponsibility.

Despite all of these caveats, a discussion of organizational alternatives, particularly as these apply to libraries, is useful. After many years of assumed "perfection," library structures are being reexamined and many are being changed. These changes result from different patron attitudes and expectations and, more importantly, from an acceleration of expected service responses. Changes are required because today's (and most certainly tomorrow's) library is heavily dependent on outside agencies and support services, and on increasingly sophisticated technology. These interactions require specialized skills and may suggest organizational changes.

TYPES OF ORGANIZATIONAL STRUCTURES

Management theorists tell us that there are five basic ways of grouping employees for the performance of useful work: by function, by geographic location, by product, by customer or client and by number of people. Almost every possible approach has its advantages and disadvantages. If personnel management problems were easily solved, the topic would not be nearly as controversial. The reader is warned against the profusion of articles that promise "the solution"; this book will make no such claim.

By Function

The most common organizational structure in the traditional library is a clustering by function. People who perform similar work are located in one unit. Library reference and cataloging departments are obvious examples of functional organization.

Organizational clustering by function provides the efficiency and expertise of occupational specialization and it facilitates training. It also promotes cooperation because similar interests and values are grouped together. Finally, it allows for the efficient use of machinery and avoids equipment duplication. While libraries are not as heavily equipment-dominated as manufacturing organizations, it can be easily seen that the scheduling of OCLC terminals is simplified if all of its users work in the same physical area.

Arrangement by function also has disadvantages, and these clearly apply to libraries. Clustering by function promotes insular and narrow viewpoints, in which there is frequently a failure to come to grips with or even see overall organizational problems or issues. Solutions are seen only in terms of the group's own needs.

Perhaps an obvious illustration would be a cataloging department that concerns itself exclusively with the quality of the cataloging being performed and not with the question of why cataloging takes place. Consideration of this more fundamental question would lead to the need for determining what qualitative standards are necessary for the meeting of objectives. Many libraries are characterized by a lack of overall organizational objectives which individuals can identify and to which they can subscribe. When this occurs, functional group objectives become paramount.

By Geographic Location

A second organizational arrangement is by geographic location. In academic and public library systems, the development of branch libraries represents the most obvious example of this phenomenon. The relationship between these branches and the central body frequently becomes a continuing power struggle. The heads of geographically isolated units understandably want control over their own affairs, and are usually supported in this striving by their user communities.

As an example, academic branch librarians generally prefer to complete their own interlibrary loan transactions, partly because they believe they can do so faster and can more readily identify likely loan sources. Primarily, however, they want this authority because they have the responsibility for explaining to disgruntled users why the material has still not arrived at the library.

Geographic dispersal is generally opposed on the principle that it leads to redundancy and duplication, and this is clearly true. However, there are situations for which even redundancy or duplication is worthwhile because these are providing rapidity of service, assurance of access, or convenience not otherwise assured. When this is the choice, additional resources must be provided. Greater convenience frequently implies greater cost.

Many large academic and public library systems operate with some level of geographic dispersal, with academic libraries more inclined to transfer authority to the branch unit head. This results primarily from the fact that the users at academic geographically dispersed locations have more power than public library branch users. An extreme example of library geographic dispersal is frequently found in special libraries, in which local library personnel often report directly to local management; any cooperation with central management policy is limited to good will (if any) on the part of local management.

By Product

The third organizational approach, by product, has little application for libraries. Manufacturing organizations often find this approach attractive because it provides a unified accountability for performance. At the same time, it frequently leads to a duplication of effort, such as that which occurs when models of the same automobile are assembled in more than one plant, under the auspices of managers who perceive their fellow managers as rivals.

By Customer or Client

The fourth approach, by customer or client, is most directly applicable to marketing organizations, but it does have some relevance for libraries. In many cases, this approach overlaps the geographic location approach, because specialized customer groups can also be separately housed. The most immediate library example concerns law and medical libraries in academic institutions which, unlike branch libraries serving chemistry, education or music, usually report directly to their client community with, at best, a consulting relationship with the main library.

Library organization by client seems to occur for only one reason: when the client community is sufficiently interested to want control over its library and strong enough to have its way, as with law and medicine.

By Number of People

The fifth and last fundamental approach, by number of people, has no application for libraries, except perhaps insofar as typing or stenographic pool organizations are established. This model is most appropriate for the organization of armed forces, which is based directly on the size of the unit, be it a squad, platoon, company, battalion, regiment or division.

LINE VS. STAFF FUNCTIONS

The reader will already have noted that few organizations, and certainly few libraries, are pure examples of a single organizational model. Many operate in combinations of two or more structures; for example, projects may be established which in effect combine characteristics of functional or product structure. These can be staff projects, under which people are pulled together as a committee or team for the resolution of a specific issue or problem.

They can also be line projects, under which individuals are assigned temporarily to specific tasks other than those which they normally perform. This can occur through a temporary physical relocation, or through the process of giving an individual still working at his or her own desk an overriding assignment of presumably greater priority. Unless an arrangement is made with and through the supervisor normally responsible for scheduling that individual's work, problems can ensue.

These examples bring into focus the classic relationship between line and staff functions, a relationship fraught with potential difficulties. Two classical library staff functions—personnel and systems—will be discussed later in this chapter.

A line management relationship, under which each individual works directly for one boss, is the classic and simplest relationship. In small organizations it is the only relationship. A library with a staff of five would almost certainly have one supervisor and four subordinates who reported directly to that one individual, although the staff members would have different rates of pay and prestige. In such organizations there is no necessity to define additional hierarchical relationships.

Perhaps paradoxically, in larger organizations based on the bureaucratic model of organizational structure to be described later, it becomes essential to do so. If an organization has 50 or 100 employees, it becomes equally important not only for each employee to know who the supervisor is, but also to know who it is *not,* to avoid overlapping and contradictory instructions.

The bureaucratic line management model, on which most library organization is still based, has many shortcomings. However, it has the great advantage of simplicity and clarity. Individuals do indeed need to know and insist on knowing who their supervisors are, which individuals are entitled to give them instructions and which ones are not.

The development of staff functions not directly connected with the overall direction taken by an organization in its day-today operations results from both growth and complexity. Staff support services that perform functions are sometimes difficult to differentiate from line function divisions. This can cause problems when the staff support service takes on the characteristics of a full-fledged organizational body with its own goals and objectives, although it presumably is not supposed to have any. Such is the case when personnel, accounting and purchasing departments insist on adherence to procedures which may provide orderliness and efficiency, but which have no direct relevance to the purpose for which these departments were established.

All libraries must deal with staff support services such as these, and in many cases these relationships cause the greatest difficulty for the library manager trying to get the library's objectives met. However, most libraries do not contain such service divisions. They are more likely to have staff specialists, employed for their particular expertise.

There is always the inherent potential for conflict between staff services and line supervisors. The former are likely to insist that things be done properly and efficiently. The latter often recognize their primary responsibility is to see to it that things get done and do not care how. Occasionally a line supervisor has a commitment to the preservation of the *status quo,* and therefore has an interest in seeing that things do *not* get done. This balance of relationships is not necessarily unhealthy when it provides a variety of viewpoints for higher levels of management, but it must never be allowed to disintegrate into bickering and personal clashes.

STRUCTURAL CHANGES IN LIBRARIES TODAY

Libraries are indeed changing, in part because of the impact of new technology, in part because of an awakening sense of involvement of staff, both professional and clerical. However, the primary reason for this change is the simple fact that a failure to change is untenable. Our resources no longer meet our needs as we have traditionally defined our objectives. We have tried to avoid the implementation of cuts by delays, and to absorb them by asking our staff members to work harder and accomplish more. That does not work, as we should have known all along it would not work.

For whatever reason, and rarely because of enthusiasm on the part of administrators, librarians are moving away from the traditional, bureaucratic model and toward organic systems. These represent polarized approaches and in practice few organizations find success with either model in its purest form. A middle ground incorporating some of each is usually arrived at, most frequently through pragmatism, sometimes through trial and error, rarely through theoretical formulation.

Organic Systems

Organic systems are characterized by job definitions of less narrowness and rigidity than those in bureaucratic systems and there is also less emphasis on conformity to rules. Employees share, or at least are expected to share, a commitment to overall goals beyond their own job boundaries. This does not occur automatically, but it is fundamental to the success of any personnel management system.

In organically oriented systems, authority and power are delegated and dispersed, and managers are not viewed as omniscient any more than omnipotent. Communication is horizontal and diagonal as well as vertical, and consists more of advice, information and suggestions than of direct orders. Collaboration and consultancy are emphasized, and the organization chart features a wider span of control; i.e., each supervisor has responsibility for a greater number of subordinates and, as a result, the number of management levels is reduced. Finally, individual staff members are encouraged to take responsibility for solving problems.

The organic system corresponds far more closely than the bureaucratic system to the optimistic view of mankind as championed by the behavioral scientists of the last 30 years. It is a far more attractive concept than bureaucratic management, and precisely because of this, must be approached with extreme caution. Various modifications which incorporate organic systems theory into the bureaucratic model may indeed work. It is likely that at least some change is essential. However, changes will not work simply because we want them to, and any such assumption is not only idealistic, it is naive and wrong. A commitment to the overall benefit of the library is interpreted differently by each participant. The word "cooperation," without further constraints or definitions, is usually understood to mean "your doing things as I have proposed them."

In some sense, the modification of traditional library structure poses risks at least as great as the potential benefits. However, they are risks which must be taken, because retention of the bureaucratic *status quo* is for most libraries now unendurable.

The Columbia University Libraries Model

A shift from a bureaucratic to a more organic systems model has occurred at the Columbia University Libraries. This resulted in response to a study undertaken by Booz, Allen & Hamilton, Inc., with support from the Association of Research Libraries, the American Council on Education and the Council on Library Resources. (The full report is available in published form and will only be summarized here.[1]) The consultants recommended specific alternatives to the traditional technical services/reader services division of authority and responsibility so prevalent in most larger libraries. Instead, Booz, Allen recommended organization into five major units:

1) A Resources Group, including collection development, faculty and research liaison, and bibliographic control.

2) A Services Group, focusing on first-line user services subdivided according to three major subject groupings of humanities, social sciences and science.

3) A Support Group, including records and materials processing as well as business services.

4) A Personnel Office.

5) A Planning Office to take responsibility for both program planning and budgeting.

The report is at this writing more than 10 years old, but even today it represents the most systematic approach to the restructuring of a traditional library system. No other library system has since copied these recommendations in whole or in major part. This is prudent, since no plan devised for the conditions at one library can be adopted directly for any other. However, the concepts of organizational decentralization have taken hold, and in the next few years we can expect to see an increasing number of libraries attempt to shorten the decision-making process.

How Organic Systems Will Develop

Some library directors will attempt to streamline decision making through the relatively simple step of allowing branch librarians to take full responsibility for requesting and obtaining material on interlibrary loan, and perhaps also for lending materials from their own collections. Others are considering the far more radical step of decentralizing all original cataloging. This will leave only the process of adapting records from national bibliographic files without intellectual review as a centralized semi-clerical function. Original cataloging, these library directors propose, will be performed in closer physical and intellectual contact with the reference and bibliographic staffs who use this material. It is too early to determine whether or not all, or even many, of these proposed changes will be effective, but they are consistent with the emphases of organic organization theory and the closer involvement of individual staff members in both decisions and responsibilities concerning their work.

ORGANIZING STAFF FUNCTIONS

Even a casual examination of the major recommendations of the Columbia University study will disclose a strong emphasis on the development of staff functions performed on a centralized basis. The staff functions in question are personnel administration and systems planning. They are proposed as centralized activities both because they represent levels of expertise which cannot be replicated at the local supervisory level, and because such planning and decisions are viewed as necessary on an overall and consistent basis.

The development of staff (as opposed to line) functions in libraries is almost immediately thought of as relating to personnel activities. Personnel departments exist as staff activities in virtually all larger public and academic libraries, even when an outside parent body (such as a municipal government or university administration) also has personnel management responsibilities. Special libraries, by contrast, are rarely large enough to warrant a separate personnel function and depend on the larger organization for this service.

The implementation of staff support services is usually both a factor of size and complexity on the one hand, and of specialized skills and knowledge on the other. It is this second set of criteria which has largely been responsible for the emergence of library systems development officers as the second most common staff activity. By and large, most libraries have no other designated staff functions, although the Columbia University study suggests the centralization of both budgeting and planning as a specific staff activity.

Occasionally, a library organization chart will indicate a position specified as "assistant to...," which clearly identifies it as a staff rather than a line position. An assistant to someone draws authority specifically from that of the superior and exercises it completely at the discretion of that individual. In some instances such "assistants to" perform very specific and necessary jobs which are clearly understood by everyone and which do not interact or conflict with the normal daily tasks performed within the organization. Planning a special conference or celebration might be the kind of task assignment delegated to such an assistant.

In other instances, the title unfortunately designates an individual who had to be removed from the line organization for reasons of organizational policy or ineffectiveness, but who is being kept within the library, at least for the present. For such individuals the title "assistant to" can be rather meaningless and is quickly dismissed as such by other individuals in the organization.

Since the authority of a staff support service is rarely spelled out in detail, and is not as obviously apparent as line control over certain numbers of subordinates or financial resources, some staff services are extremely weak and represent little authority. Others, by contrast, represent a great deal of power and authority, acquired either by direct delegation from the superior official or by the persuasive or argumentative skills of the staff incumbent.

An excess in either direction is undesirable. Since it is the purpose of a staff function to provide specialized expertise or additional insights for the decision process, any administrator who either permits staff support services to dominate, or who allows line supervisors to treat staff personnel as clerical lackeys, is losing most of the advantages which such an environment provides. The interaction of line and staff activities in addressing a particular problem permits the expression of what may be diverse viewpoints. It also allows the higher level manager a broader range of counsel.

THE INTERRELATIONSHIP OF LINE AND STAFF WORKERS

Viewpoints and priorities of staff and line personnel are not automatically antagonistic, but they can frequently start from that premise. A healthy organizational environment permits room for negotiation or compromise. At the very least, it permits the higher level manager to hear the free expression of both viewpoints.

The reason for potential antagonism is that the staff support division examines the needs and priorities of the whole organization, while line supervisors quite properly interpret their responsibilities as meeting the specific objectives established for their units. While they have no quarrel with overall organizational objectives, as long as these do not conflict with their own targets, they recognize quite clearly and correctly that their own rewards will come in direct relationship to what they and their units accomplish and not necessarily to what others accomplish.

Personnel Decisions

A line supervisor can, for example, quite clearly identify the one person who should be hired, promoted or transferred to meet the unit's specific needs. The staff personnel officer, by contrast, must look at overall policy, overriding needs and even legal restrictions. The resolution to this potential conflict may come through an arbitrary edict supporting one or the other viewpoint. Sometimes this is ultimately necessary, but it should be avoided where possible. It is far preferable to give all subordinates a similar stake in the achievement of overall goals.

Fundamentally, in any management decision environment, individuals will choose what they perceive as best for them as the appropriate course of action. They will then develop a rationalization to demonstrate that this course is also best for the organization at large. This is an important point to which this book will return repeatedly. When people do things willingly, it is because they perceive it as advantageous for the organization, which means that they consider it advantageous or at least not threatening to them.

This point must be kept in mind when we attempt to "persuade" a supervisor to accept a lesser choice in filling a vacancy. Supervisors already know the risk implicit in such action—i.e., that the work will not be done as well, and that they will be blamed. If there are advantages to them within this situation, these need to be spelled out more clearly. The injunction to agree "for the benefit of the larger organization" is sometimes ultimately necessary, but it is used far too frequently and usually received with a large dose of cynicism.

Systems Analysis and Programming

The clash of two distinct value systems becomes even clearer in the way line employees perceive the staff activities performed by systems analysts and programmers. Some employees in any library will be predisposed to automation while others will view such activities with fear and even loathing. To some extent such attitudes can be changed through continuing education, such as is provided by internal workshops and seminars, and to some extent negative attitudes must be recognized and overridden. Of greatest concern to an individual is the question of what systems development and automation will do to his or her own job—to its quality and even its continuance.

The fear of being replaced by automation is particularly prevalent today because there is much in the general literature which describes the elimination of jobs by machines. Some of it is true, but much of it is exaggerated. Concerns are also heightened by the suggestion that the planned mechanization "will pay for itself." If that payout comes through greater accomplishments by the same number of people, that point must be made. If not, employees will almost automatically assume that the savings will come at the expense of their own jobs. In the absence of specific information, individuals have an almost infallible way of inventing a scenario which is far worse than anything which could possibly happen. That, of course, is the ultimate danger of rumors.

If automation is to result in the elimination of positions, the individuals involved can hardly be expected to cooperate to their own detriment. Fortunately, this rarely occurs, in part because of tenure and seniority protection, and in part because staff attrition is generally considered preferable as a tool for personnel reductions.

Also of major concern to employees is the question of what will happen to their jobs as a result of the proposed changes. Will they be enriched and more interesting, perhaps at a higher rate of pay? Will they be more routine and mundane and perhaps isolated from contact with others? Will they require skills they presently do not possess, and how are these new skills to be acquired?

All of these questions will receive far greater attention in the specific chapter devoted to the implementation of technology in libraries. At this point, in the consideration of the relationship between staff and line activities, note just that such a mix is not automatically or even normally positive or pleasant. It can and should be, but this will occur only as a result of careful planning and communication.

PERSONNEL FUNCTIONS WITHIN THE LIBRARY STRUCTURE

The functions of personnel organizations are generally well known and for the reader interested in greater detail are available in a wealth of management publications. Personnel administration, a relatively young discipline dating back perhaps 50 years, originally evolved as a protective device to provide a consistent response to the threat of unionization. It is only in the last 25 years, in keeping with the development of more humanistic and optimistic personnel management concepts, that the potentially positive and contributory aspects of a strong personnel staff organization have been recognized.

Functions assigned to personnel departments include a variety of activities, not all of which are relevant to libraries and not all invariably focused on a staff group. From the list of potential activities itemized below, it can be seen that personnel departments can be large and powerful. In other situations they can have much narrower duties, focused essentially on the selection and hiring process, and on the administration of a wage and salary policy. However, the recognition that some overall staff coordination in this area is desirable is now widely accepted.

Libraries that do not have their own personnel staff departments are invariably subject to the scrutiny of such a group in the parent body. Personnel activities are viewed correctly as far too important to permit the *laissez-faire* approach common before the 20th century, and which many line supervisors would probably secretly prefer. Personnel functions include:

- Help in the selection of employees. Ideally, this is a cooperative process involving agreement between the staff and line divisions. When supervisors can hire anyone they want, or when personnel departments arbitrarily shove unwanted candidates at the direct supervisor, something is wrong.

- Orientation and training. The first of these is usually dealt with directly by the personnel department; the second is frequently a combined and cooperative effort.

- Performance appraisal. While the appraisal itself is made by the line supervisor, the personnel organization is responsible for both a consistent evaluation process and for an analysis and interpretation of its results.

- The development and monitoring of pay increase policies. Directives as to actual amounts and procedures may come from higher-level management, but the personnel department is usually responsible for monitoring both fairness and consistency. It is inconsistency, rather than the actual amount, that is normally the greatest source of irritation and complaint.

- The settling of complaints. Subordinates' grievances may or may not be valid, and it is important to treat them seriously. In most line function situations individuals run a considerable risk in voicing a complaint, particularly when it is against their supervisor. This role of ombudsman is a particularly important one in the absence of a union, or of an otherwise clearly spelled out grievance procedure.

- The handling of personnel shifts, including promotions, transfers and, if necessary, ultimate layoffs. Since these transactions involve the aspirations, hopes and fears of all staff members, it is essential that the process be carried out with a fairness and balance which is understood and accepted. The role of the direct supervisor in this process will be examined in Chapter 9 in much greater detail.

In summary, it should be noted that the development of staff functions in libraries, as in other organizations, results from the need to establish consistency, to undertake overall planning, and to share scarce talents and needs. Staff and line functions do not mix easily in organizations which, despite ongoing changes, are still largely bureaucratic and hierarchical. Supervisors will frequently resent intrusions by staff personnel who, they argue, have authority but no responsibility. The role of higher management in clarifying tasks and relationships, and in assuaging fears and providing reassurance, is crucial.

NOTES

1. Booz, Allen, and Hamilton, Inc., *Organization and Staffing of the Libraries of Columbia University. A Case Study* (Westport, CT: Redgrave Information Resources Corp., 1973).

3

Reconciling Organizational and Individual Objectives

GOALS ARE NOT ENOUGH

While some management theorists use the terms goals and objectives interchangeably, in this book a clear distinction will be made between the two. Goals are statements of overall purpose and philosophy which frequently represent ideals. Statements such as "The purpose of this library is to provide the greatest possible level of service to all members of the community," or "The goal of the library is to support the research and teaching mission of the university," are examples of goals. They will be easily recognized by the reader, because virtually all libraries have goals.

Valuable as goals are, their shortcomings for management planning are immediately apparent. What is the "greatest possible level of service?" How do we know when we are indeed supporting the research and teaching mission of the university adequately? Can we ever know, and can we ever accomplish that goal? It is not likely.

In one sense goals are slogans, and while slogans can serve to inspire, their impact is limited. Libraries cannot build their programs and their priorities on goals alone, because these provide no solid foundation. When libraries deal only in the discussion of goals, they create the impression characterized by Robert Munn[1] of being "bottomless pits." Management quickly gets the idea that no matter how obliging one is in meeting library demands, librarians will never be satisfied. Therefore, far from spurring these administrators to make a greater effort to provide requested funding or more staff, it tends to discourage them. Since librarians will never be satisfied, since the collection will never be "adequate," since we will never have served everyone who is a potential client, what, they argue, is the use of even trying?

THE NEED FOR FINITE ACCOMPLISHMENTS

In return for generosity, those requesting funds promise not only to be grateful, but also to give the donor credit for a finite accomplishment. It is generally recognized that appeals for new library buildings, either in academic or public settings, tend to be met more responsively than requests for more staff or for more books. This is precisely because a building is a finite need and a finite accomplishment. Once it is finished, we no longer have to keep building it, and we can also get credit for what we have accomplished.

This is an important distinction in human motivation, and one that will be stressed later in more detail. Individuals, be they mayors or boards of trustees on the one hand, or library file clerks on the other, need the sense of accomplishment which comes from successfully completing a task or achieving a goal. Library managers who fail to recognize that need will be in serious difficulty.

It is largely a lack of understanding of these needs that causes many of the difficulties encountered by the library profession. It is only a slight exaggeration to state that our appeals to Congress for funds to support and enhance the Library Services and Construction Act or the library funding provisions of the Higher Education Act are requests for money "to make things slightly less rotten than they are at present." They will, of course, still be rotten. Funding will still be inadequate, and the goal will still be unmet. It should not be surprising, then, that our appeals are not enthusiastically received.

When NASA asked for funds in the 1960s, it promised to put a man on the moon before the end of the decade, and it kept that promise. The space agency's funding difficulties since that time result in large part from the fact that its later requests have been less tied to specifically measurable and politically desirable objectives, and have therefore been less enthusiastically embraced. The lesson should not be lost on librarians.

USING MEASURABLE OBJECTIVES

Goals require a further refinement and articulation in the form of objectives. These are statements proposing what is to be accomplished, and within what time frame. Objectives are quantifiable and they are measurable. The statement, "We intend to increase book circulation to the Hispanic community served by this branch library by 30% over the next two years," is an objective. Whether or not it is a valid objective obviously cannot be determined in this abstract context, but if it valid, it then becomes a target which can be easily recognized by library administrators, library employees and those who wield ultimate power over the library.

If an objective cannot be met, or if no way of meeting it can be envisioned, it should be withdrawn. Otherwise, it stands as a reminder of unkept promises and implied inefficiency which will turn the most motivated staff into self-doubting defeatists. Objectives should be important, they should be worthwhile and *they should be achievable.* If management is perceived as doubting either the validity or the practicality of objectives, staff members will pick up on this.

It is not always easy to achieve agreement from those who exercise administrative and financial control over the library, but not only can it be done, it must be done. The recent development of concepts of "management of objective" provides the ideal vehicle for this transaction. Higher level administrators, who are only vaguely aware of a library's role, will probably settle for a statement of goals and may be willing to exempt the library from the development of objectives. It is a poor bargain for the library administrator.

Without objectives there is not only aimlessness, but also a lack of follow-up to determine the resources in dollars and staff necessary to implement those objectives. Giving librarians responsibility without resources is something administrators recognize as untenable, but that will not stop them from trying the ploy if we accept the premise. If pleasing the faculty is important to the university president, the president must be willing to bear the cost. For example, if pleasing the faculty requires the development of specific campus delivery services, either the cost of those services must be met or the objective must be withdrawn. If the latter occurs, it is necessary to clarify why the objective was withdrawn, and by whose decision.

There are several reasons for stressing the need for objectives. Libraries represent organizations whose contribution to the well-being of the community which houses them is generally assumed and appreciated, but rarely quantified. As budgetary resources decline, administrators support what they must and avoid what they can avoid.

Objectives As Motivational Tools

At a recent seminar for presidents of theological seminaries of various denominations, I asked participants if they would be content with a situation in which the library functioned within its assigned budget and yet somehow avoided offending campus power groups, in particular the faculty. These administrators agreed that they would happily settle for such an outcome, without asking any additional questions.

Their attitude is certainly understandable, but nevertheless unacceptable. The libraries in their institutions may have goals, but their only tangible objective is survival. The impact of such a scenario on a library employee, and the lack of motivation to plan or innovate, can be easily imagined. Individuals who work in such an environment have little if any motivation for achievement, since achievement has never even been defined.

Unfulfilled Objectives

Important as objectives are, it must be recognized that not all objectives can be realized. On the one hand, others may disagree as to the importance of what has been proposed. On the other hand, it is possible that there is agreement as to its importance, but an inability to provide the resources necessary for a given plan's implementation. If and when this occurs, the objective must be withdrawn, no matter how important, for the reasons discussed above.

It is probably a good idea to have *some* worthwhile projects left undone for future years. Even more important is that all remaining objectives have a reasonable chance for successful completion. All staff members should accept a commitment to this accomplishment.

The implementation of objectives requires both programs and strategies, and these in turn identify who will do what, when and with what resources. This is the purpose of the budgeting-by-objectives process. Even libraries not required to participate in this planning strategy are encouraged to do so for the benefits of their own management and staff. Assigning a task to a subordinate should be accompanied by a discussion of how the task is to be accomplished. The statement "do the best you can" is widely recognized to mean that success is not expected. The phrase "do it in your spare time" implies an understanding that it won't happen at all. People do not have spare time; and even if they did, they could not acknowledge that fact, as it would make them vulnerable to being identified as surplus.

DEFINING OBJECTIVES IN PERIODS OF DECLINE

A number of articles, including one by Bo Hedberg[2], have dealt with the mangement of decline. Decades of management writings have dealt with the management of growth, on the premise that all organizations grow and that the manager must only supervise and coordinate that growth. If an organization does not grow, these writers have suggested, the supervisor must surely be at fault.

Hedberg examines situations in which organizational funding has declined, through no fault of the operating management, and suggests that there is extreme reluctance to come to grips with the results of this change. He suggests that the initial reaction is belief that the retraction is temporary and will soon be reversed. As long as this is believed, nothing will be done, because nothing need be done. "The situation will soon right itself."

It is only after the realization that the change is not temporary has been accepted that most organizations move to a second stage. In this environment, organizations prepare to absorb the reduction in resources (or the increase in requirements without a growth in resources) by working harder. Hedberg suggests that this strategy is disastrous for two reasons. First, it concentrates on working more rapidly or more efficiently at whatever is being done, without examining whether the right thing is being done or whether the proper methods are being used. In other words, it concentrates on efficiency instead of effectivenss.

Second, and even more important, such an approach alienates the entire staff. The suggestion that more work can be absorbed if employees try harder is equivalent to the suggestion that up to now individuals have been slacking off or wasting time. Even if the premise were correct, it would be totally unacceptable to the individuals involved, because it would be tantamount to a self-indictment. The suggestion that more can be done by working harder is therefore immediately rejected. The employee now has a clear stake in proving that more work cannot possibly be absorbed, and with that aim in mind, will have no difficulty in proving it. Besides, what incentive can there possibly be for absorbing more work? If by some stretch of the imagination it really is possible and ultimately does occur, it will only encourage management to try it again.

According to Hedberg, organizations cannot come to grips with the management of decline until they accept the fact that with declining resources, objectives must change and programs must change. What those changes will entail is negotiable, and higher management may or may not want to participate. However, any suggestion that resources might change but objectives will not must be characterized as the nonsense it truly represents.

INVOLVING STAFF IN THE ATTAINMENT OF OBJECTIVES

The development of objectives in any organization represents the construction of a contract, based on plans and programs that identify resources. For the individual employee entrusted with carrying out this contract there must be a mutuality of trust and understanding based on the premise that what is being asked is both reasonable and possible. When a subordinate disagrees as to the validity of the task assignment, it must be made clear not only that management *expects* the task to be completed, but also *why* the expectation is reasonable. Credibility will flow not only from a record of successes, but from the perception on the part of the employee that the relationship between expectations and assigned resources is real, and that expectations do indeed change as resources change.

The involvement of individuals in the objectives of the organization, by giving them a stake in its success, is a relatively recent development and finds its roots in the work of behavioral scientists. It stands in direct antithesis to the management concept called "paternalism," which proposed a relaxation of job pressures and suggested that individuals need not worry about the successes or failures of the overall process, but should leave that concern to their supervisors. This concept does not work for two primary reasons: 1) subordinates usually know far more about what is really happening than we think they know or than we have told them; and 2) individuals do not like to be patronized.

The Japanese Model

There are several reasons why the development of *meaningful* and *achievable* objectives and the involvement of staff members in the evolution of these objectives and their achievement are important:

1) Human beings are goal-directed. People must have a purpose. They must have something to work toward, and announced objectives and targets provide meaning for them.

2) Objectives serve as standards against which work can be measured. As Chapter 9, which deals with performance evaluation, indicates, individuals do not resent performance evaluation; indeed, they welcome and demand it. They resent what they consider as meaningless and arbitrary criteria and rankings.

3) If individuals understand and accept the objectives, there is less need to control their work and their behavior. Voluntary coordination and cooperation are always preferable to enforced discipline, and self-regulation is the best kind of regulation.

4) Objectives stand as guidelines for the organization. They establish the concept of a team effort, with each individual seeing his or her role as a member of that team.

These concepts form the basis of the Japanese organizational structure whose success we have come to admire. Acceptance of this approach comes almost automatically in Japan. It comes less easily in the United States. Japanese workers accept from the start the premise that they must do a good job, because the overall success of the organization depends on each individual effort. The Japanese worker therefore considers his work to be not just important, but crucial. This not only causes him to work harder, but also to feel good about his work.

Encouraging Personal Responsibility

It is exactly this same feeling of personal responsibility which we are now endeavoring to instill through such mechanisms as quality control circles, work teams designed to bring employees closer to the ultimate outcome of their labors, and the development of objectives accompanied by participation at all levels. The historic bureaucratic hierarchical model of organization, ideally suited to the specific control of the work process and to the clear identification of direct authority—and therefore attractive to at least the ordering/processing assembly line-type functions common in libraries—fails in this regard. Library catalogers are often regarded as particularly alienated from the overall objectives of the library, because they see little relationship between what they do and what the library accomplishes. They question whether their cataloging more or their cataloging more carefully will make a difference.

Because catalogers see no organizational objectives which relate to them, they have, in self-defense, developed their own objectives and their own ground rules. As mentioned before, individuals like to play games, and they like a chance to win. If they think they have a fair chance of winning, and that their effort can make a difference, they will work harder.

Japanese workers instinctively accept the premise that management knows best; Americans, used to regarding management and labor as enemies (a notion promulgated by both parties), still have to be shown. Two brief examples from the writer's personal experience and observation will suffice to make the point.

In one organizational setting, a manager was able to reduce individual absenteeism by the simple practice of calculating attendance rates as percentages by departments, and then posting the results monthly as though they were sports standings. There was a noticeable amount of self-policing. Responsible employees made it clear to those with heavy and suspicious absences that they resented their departments languishing in last place in the rankings because some people were not trying.

In another example, a library director found that assigning responsibility for specific parts of the collection to individual stack attendants improved performance. These employees were told that they carried a heavy and important burden, because if they were absent no one was as qualified to do their work and organizational performance would suffer. As might be expected, the attendants rose to the challenge. Moreover, as they worked harder and more responsibly, because they had accepted the organization's objectives as reasonable and understood their important part in achieving them, their morale increased.

This should not be surprising. We have observed for some time that those individuals who accomplish the least and get away with it are not at all pleased by this success. They are also the most alienated and unhappy.

Caveats about the Japanese Model

The relationship described in the preceding paragraphs should work in any organizational environment not already poisoned by mistrust between supervisor and subordinates, or demoralized by the belief that expectations are unreasonable and arbitrary. The acceptance of that relationship is the cornerstone of the Japanese success.

At the same time, there are differences between Japanese and American cultures, and it would be a mistake to simply assume that Japanese approaches can be transferred without modification. Japanese workers, in accepting the importance of their own responsibility, also accept the premise that managers are more knowledgeable and more powerful. The presumption that anyone appointed as a supervisor obviously knows more is not automatically accepted in this country. Here, managers are expected to justify and explain their decisions and instructions. The question *why*? is rarely asked in many societies. It is constantly asked in the

American industrial and library world. It must be satisfactorily answered if cooperation is expected.

THE NEED FOR PERSONAL FULFILLMENT

The preceding sections have dealt with the need to develop, promulgate and explain organizational objectives so that individual employees accept these as their own. However, each worker also has a second set of objectives that he or she brings to the workplace, and which also governs behavior—the set of personal fulfillment needs. These two sets of objectives must be reconciled successfully, but this is not as difficult as it may seem as long as the existence of two distinct sets of objectives is recognized.

There is nothing inherently antagonistic between these two sets. In fact, the sensitive manager can help create an environment in which these are mutually supportive. The need to create such an environment makes personnel management such an individualized activity. Policies are necessary generalizations, but supervision is an individual practice geared to a unique relationship. Creating such an atmosphere takes time and requires sensitivity, but it is worth it.

Maslow's Hierarchy of Needs

The psychologist Abraham Maslow[3] promulgated his widely acclaimed theory of rank ordering of human priorities and needs 30 years ago, but his writings still have the same vitality today.

According to Maslow, there is a definite rank-order priority of human needs. Until the more basic wants are fulfilled, a person will not strive to meet higher needs. However, when basic needs are met, individuals will move on to the next category. Maslow identified five hierarchical levels of need:

1) Physiological needs (such as food and shelter).

2) Safety, stability and security.

3) "Belongingness" and love.

4) Self-esteem and the esteem of others.

5) Self-actualization, self-realization and self-accomplishment.

The implications of this hierarchy are important for an understanding of individual behavior. If a person has barely enough food, water and shelter to survive, his entire energies are devoted to staying alive. As we have learned, it is difficult to preach parliamentary democracy to individuals who are hungry, and expect them to care.

However, as various needs are satisfied, their fulfillment no longer motivates the individual. He concentrates on higher-level needs, which are less concrete. While a person can have "enough" food, more recognition, more praise and more status are always desirable.

Recent experiences in the economic sector have shown that the hierarchical flow is also reversible. When job security is at stake, other issues, including levels of salary, become less important, and club activities and other fringe benefits become luxuries. However, as soon as job security is regained, we once again focus on other issues.

Applying Maslow's Theories

There are important lessons to be learned from Maslow's postulation of need hierarchies. For one thing, it becomes obvious that simply trying to give people what they want produces very little of benefit in the work environment. Expectations can always expand more rapidly than rewards. It is widely known that salary increases, for example, no matter how generous, rarely act as any sort of motivator for a prolonged time. This is because the expectation of increased worth will have preceded the delivery. The individual being given a 20% raise may respond gratefully and courteously, but inwardly the reaction is "it's about time."

Those behavioral scientists who suggested that increased benefits and responsiveness to human needs would improve organizational performance were as simplistic as those who believed that individuals worked only for economic gain. Employees who have the benefit of dental insurance are indeed healthier, and that may be reason enough to provide it. However, having it will not cause them to work more willingly. As Maslow's hierarchy clearly implies, after having a benefit for several months, individuals absorb it as an absolute right and move on to the next unfulfilled want.

The point of this explanation is not to suggest that library managers treat their subordinates harshly or deprive them of benefits. It is rather to counter some of the arguments advanced, particularly in the humanistic literature, that ultimate happiness (assuming we could define it) produces ultimate performance. Librarians have been particularly vulnerable to such arguments.

THE PROCESS OF BEING FAIR

Management, in libraries as elsewhere, is the process of being fair, not the process of being liked. There is nothing wrong with being liked, but being fair, as well as consistent, is more important. Ultimately, any manager has two fundamental responsibilities in the area of personnel administration. The manager is responsible for assuring that the organization for which he or she works receives a fair return for its expenditure. In other words, the manager must see that the organization is treated fairly by its employees. The manager is also responsible for seeing that subordinates are treated fairly by the organization. These two requirements are not contradictory. In fact, they are complementary.

While any attempt to completely implement Maslow's hierarchy of needs pyramid is doomed to failure, a manager who is reasonable in his expectations and demands has a greater chance of success than one who is arbitrary and tyrannical. The need to determine what is "reasonable" is affected by many factors. We *do* have the responsibility for meeting the most basic of physical needs. This is why the law sets minimum wages, quite separately from the question of whether or not the individuals earning these salaries are "worth it."

Beyond this, reasonableness emerges from a series of negotiations and compromises. All but the most reckless recognize that there are limits to what can be accomplished, and we look for equity within this process. Employees would not, of course, object to being treated better than the norm, but would bitterly resent being treated worse than the norm. Such treatment is unfair, and nothing will destroy morale more quickly.

If public library employees complain that it is not fair that they have to work on Saturday without extra pay, while other municipal employees who work on the weekend or in the evening get paid at time-and-a-half rates, they are absolutely correct. In such a situation the options for the public library director are limited, but nevertheless clear. The director can point out to the municipal administration that: a) all municipal employees should get paid extra for Saturday work; b) no municipal employees should get paid extra for Saturday work; or c) the library should be closed on the weekend because of a failure to implement either options a) or b). If all of the above seems heretical, it may be because the courage needed to be a good manager is a rare commodity.

Ignoring the needs of the organization in favor of popularity is also not the answer. This approach can never succeed. As Maslow has shown, the attempt to satisfy "needs" is endless. The appropriate actions are based on a process of communication designed to identify what is fair, what is equitable and what is consistent. Weakness, vacillation or the currying of affection do not provide solutions. Balance and confidence do.

Not surprisingly, in such an environment, characterized by certainty and understanding, morale and a sense of purpose flourish. By contrast, many studies have shown that the organizations in which the least is accomplished are also those which evidence lowest morale. In postulating that there was not an irreconcilable difference between the objectives of management and those of subordinates, Frederick Taylor was absolutely correct. When there is animosity or suspicion, or when one group totally dominates the other, everyone suffers and everyone is miserable.

RECOGNIZING INDIVIDUAL DIFFERENCES

The preceding paragraphs have addressed overall individual needs and desires, and how these should be dealt with. To some extent, they must be dealt with consistently. Maslow postulates that needs hierarchies work similarly for all individuals. However, in attempting to reconcile individual behavior to the recognition and acceptance of library objectives as spelled out in plans and programs, any sensitive manager must also recognize that each individual employee brings to the job a unique set of personal goals and objectives. It is these which must be reconciled to the organizational agenda, and it is this process which requires the greatest effort and sensitivity on the part of the manager.

This is necessary because no two individuals are the same, and no two people will want the same things and respond to the same stimuli. It is this complexity that makes personnel supervision difficult, and which undermines any attempts at generalizing.

To some extent, the sweeping "truisms" promulgated by management theorists have served us badly. This chapter will consider only two of these—"job rotation" and "participative management"—but readers can certainly add their own. These concepts will be examined in greater detail in later chapters, but for the moment it is worth noting simply that both of them have been accepted in the management literature in general and the library literature in particular as "good things." As generalizations perhaps applicable to a majority of individuals, they may indeed be good. That would be of little consolation, however, to those whom they do not serve.

The mere fact that participative management appeared to be a positive value to those who enunciated the concept, or even that it may appear so to most readers of this book, is fundamentally irrelevant. It is irrelevant because the validity of such a concept must be determined for each individual employee. In turn, that determination will hinge on the personal goals and objectives that each person brings with him or her to the workplace every morning. It is this which the manager must identify, recognize and deal with.

The manager in a library, as in any organizational setting, must deal with individual objectives on two levels. The first, and most consistent, is in the establishment for each employee of personal work objectives which provide motivation, a sense of participation, a feeling of accomplishment and an aura of importance. It is when individuals see what difference their performance makes in terms of the overall whole that their own attitude responds positively. It is difficult to get members of a team who never get into the game to maintain a sense of enthusiasm. Similarly, it is difficult to get individuals with a headache to come to work rather than call in sick if they perceive no difference between their attendance and absence. Objective-setting at this level is far from simple, but it is at least fairly standardized.

Sensitivity and judgment come into play on the second and more personal level. Although Maslow's hierarchy of needs provides some useful guidelines as to priorities, specific rankings differ. Although it can be argued that probably all individuals would rather have good pay than be poorly remunerated, the importance of this factor is very much of a variable in human behavior.

Differences in Personal Motivations

Individuals who combat oil rig fires or fight mercenary wars are probably more highly motivated by the need for adventure and the search for tangible and financial rewards than are most librarians. For someone who has unpaid bills and ill-clothed children, however, salary is likely to be a crucial consideration. Thus, while all of us are pleased at the recognition and confirmation of good performance that increased salaries bring, some are more fundamentally affected by this reward than others.

For many individuals job security is the paramount benefit. The trade-off in value systems is quickly apparent when we see industrial workers take pay cuts to retain their jobs. That is, most of them appear to prefer security to higher pay *if they must choose.* Security is such a critical component of many personal value systems that unions have recognized that the seniority system for both promotion and termination (as opposed to a system based on job performance) has tremendous emotional appeal. It is predictable and offers few surprises. As long as there are others with less seniority, workers' jobs are still safe.

Security has traditionally been one of the primary attractions for the library profession. For many years librarians recognized that they would not be paid as well as others in the job force, yet they also knew that they had ironclad security. Many Civil Service workers make the same conscious or unconscious swap. It is when these individuals learn that the security they had considered fundamental no longer protects them—that tenured faculty members and full-status librarians are not immune to personnel reductions—that they really feel betrayed.

Another value system category of greater importance to some than to others is the opportunity for advancement and growth. This characteristic is found to some extent in all work groups, but probably to a much greater extent in sales than in librarianship. Where this becomes a primary driving force for individual motivation, it must be recognized.

Ambitious individuals are useful to have, but only if there are opportunities for advancement and if the candidate's capabilities have some relationship to his or her ambitions. By contrast, others (frequently those most concerned with safety and security) are not interested in promotion and may view it as a risk.

For some individuals an interesting and pleasant workplace is paramount. For others it is the existence of safe and healthful working conditions. For example, an individual under doctor's orders to seek a dry, warm climate will almost certainly put that requirement above all others. By contrast, an individual wholly committed to activities such as scouting or competitive bowling leagues may well demand that there be no weekend work and no evening overtime. For such individuals, promotions to positions of higher pay and prestige, which eliminate that safeguard, provide little, if any, satisfaction.

The list of individual preferences is almost endless. Some persons consider it important to have interesting work with a variety of challenges and working experiences. Others feel threatened by an environment in which they are forced to encounter new experiences, or in which a great deal of interpretation or decision making is required.

It can be quickly seen that for one group the concept of job enrichment or job rotation would not only be an asset but perhaps an absolute requirement. For others, such a condition would provide a real threat, and might force them to consider leaving.

Finally, the concept of participation in the decision process, quite inexactly called "participative management" (in reality it is at best participative input to the management process), is embraced by some and feared by others.

WHEN INDIVIDUAL OBJECTIVES CANNOT BE FULFILLED

Understanding individuals' *job* objectives and individuals' *personal* objectives does not always lead to success in dealing with them. People who want to become millionaires by working in libraries are in the wrong profession. Individuals who want to be autocratic managers without the need to explain their actions are living at least 100 years too late.

When no accommodation is possible, it is important that this be realized as quickly as possible so that "something" can be done. That something may be a transfer, a resignation or a termination.

With a stubborness that belies reasonableness, some humanistic management theorists insist that all problems have solutions given the application of enough patience, effort and good will. This is not true, and when we find a problem without an acceptable accommodation, decisive action is called for. Delay and equivocation hurt the organization. They also hurt employees, by causing them to waste their time in positions from which no ultimate good can emerge.

However, these are extreme and unusual circumstances. Accommodation between organizational and individual objectives is indeed possible in most instances. Most subordinates prefer to be productively useful, because the satisfaction of meaningful work is as important to them as it is to managers. It is only when they become alienated, when they believe they have been mistreated or abused, that they look for the chance to get even by purposely performing poorly. More commonly, such alienation is not confrontational and consists largely of employees doing as little as possible, and only exactly what they are told to do. Uncaring subordinates, however, are just as disastrous for the library as a group of employees who purposely disregard or reject their assignments.

Deciding What Can Be Sacrificed

The reader will have noted that while some characteristics (good pay, cooperation, a pleasant working environment, dignified treatment) are desired by everyone, what employees are willing to concede to get them may differ widely. This point is important because, in keeping with Maslow, it is impossible to match expectations which grow and always stay one step ahead of actualization. "Happiness" is a will-o'-the-wisp which is never achievable. Reasonable accommodation is a much more realistic and perfectly acceptable goal. Since we probably cannot give everyone everything they want, we should try to give them what is most important to them, *if we can*. It is absurd to give people what they do not want simply because the manager considers it a benefit and considers it important in his or her own value system.

At the same time, just about all individuals would like some sense of control over their own personal job environment. As the Japanese have learned, this is not an abdication of management control in areas that matter. It is just plain good sense.

NOTES

1. Munn, Robert F., "The Bottomless Pit, or the Academic Library as Viewed from the Administration Building," *College and Research Libraries* 29 (January 1968):51-54.

2. Hedberg, Bo, et al., "Camping on Seesaws. Prescriptions for a Self-Designing Organization," *Administrative Sciences Quarterly* 21(1)(1976):41-65.

3. Maslow, Abraham, *Motivation and Personality* (New York: Harper & Row, 1954).

4

Adapting to Changes in Technology

Technological change in libraries is widely discussed. Many articles and books deal with the technology of online searching, networks and microcomputers. This chapter will deal with a subject that has received much less attention: how to manage technological change in libraries. It will focus particularly on how to present such change to employees.

In early writings Peter Drucker has already made the point for this approach. Technology, Drucker argues, is not about tools. It is about how people work.[1] Drucker was not talking about libraries, but some of his points are well worth repeating, because their application is general. He argued that automation is really nothing more than a conceptual extension of Frederick Taylor's theory of scientific management, and that once operations have been analyzed it turns out that in many cases they can be performed by machines. Far from being dismayed by this shift, he saw automation and other applications of technology as a shift from manual to mental work.

By and large, Drucker has been correct. However, this optimistic assessment of technological change has been of little consolation to those who performed manual work and either preferred it to mental work or were incapable of the latter.

THE NEED FOR A SYSTEMS APPROACH

Technological changes do indeed have an impact on organizational dynamics far beyond the simple exchange of one task for another. For example, the technology of automation, particularly as it applies to the multiple use of data prepared only once, requires a systems approach to the work of the whole organization. This approach means integrating a lot of activities and processes that were formerly thought of as unrelated.

The systems approach is particularly significant for libraries, for which historically very little organizational planning existed, in part because of the absence of measurable objectives. Organizational discipline is assumed to follow naturally from the setting of targets and the development of plans to achieve these targets. The lack of this discipline in libraries has long made them small enclaves in which local rules, or even instinctive judgments, held sway.

The implementation of a systems approach imposes a far stricter sense of organizational discipline. In libraries that are part of systems, specific cataloging decisions become too important to be left to the judgment of individual catalogers or even to heads of cataloging, since such decisions are part of larger-scale determinations with wider implications.

PLANNING FOR CHANGE

Automation requires planning. Planning, as Drucker has stressed, is not forecasting; in fact, it is required precisely because of our inability to forecast accurately. Nor, of course, is planning an alternative to future decision making or to the taking of risks. It is, rather, an attempt to prepare a framework for the inevitability of both decisions and risks.

Libraries are not automatically well-suited to this task. Systems structuring and planning are skills rarely taught in schools of library science and rarely demanded of newly hired personnel. There is little in the humanistic backgrounds of most librarians to prepare them for this task, and nothing hinted at in the characteristics stressed by guidance counselors.

If automation requires system-wide analysis and planning, then the absence of such processes in manual library systems will become even more damaging as they start to deal with automation. Without clear expectations of what automation is designed to accomplish, it is likely that very little will be gained.

The experience of some major academic libraries when they first began including OCLC data in the cataloging process illustrates the problem of lack of planning. The work only served to slow the cataloging activity and to increase backlogs. Catalogers were at that time using OCLC information as an additional advisory input to their own cataloging decisions. It was only when ground rules governing the acceptance and rejection of OCLC data were devised that any economic benefits could be claimed. Unfortunately, the belated imposition of such standards caused resentments, in terms of both a perceived potential loss of jobs and a loss of "quality."

Introducing Employees to the Concept of Automation

Before automation can be presented to employees in a library, it is essential that a great deal of planning first occur at management levels. It is then important that the plan be widely discussed with all members of the staff, and that these discussions address as directly and honestly as possible central concerns of both organizational and individual objectives. For the organization, the underlying questions are, "Why are we considering doing this at all?" "Are there present problems that automation is designed to address?" "Are there new objectives which can be achieved with automation that are presently outside our reach?" The answers to the latter two questions are generally in the affirmative, or at least managers think they are in the affirmative. It is essential that they also inform the members of the staff of what they believe, of why they believe it and of how the decision was reached.

Allowing for Costs and Training Time

An essential part of planning for automated library systems is to allow enough time and money. Automation rarely (although occasionally) produces tangible savings. In most cases it costs more, not only because it tends to replace cheap labor with more expensive professional labor, but also because it leads to an expectation for yet more products and services. This should be looked upon as an advantage and not a detriment by library administrators in their own dealings with their superiors. If you are going to ask for more resources, it is wise to have something to offer in return. The system of barter exists even at the highest management levels. It is more likely that the presumed benefits of automation will lie not in savings, but in increased responsiveness and in the provision of products and services not possible at all in a manual system.

Besides underestimating systems and equipment costs, managers frequently also fail to take into account the impact on individual workers and their productivity. Education and training time probably cannot be localized at the front end of the implementation. It will be continuous. The learning curve—the time it takes an individual to become fluent with a new assignment or a new procedure—is also frequently ignored. The length of the learning curve will depend on the complexity of the task and the qualification and attitude of the employee being trained, and can vary from a few hours to many months.

AUTOMATION AS A THREAT

Quite aside from what automation promises to do for the library, individuals will be concerned about what it means for them. Some change is easily explained as an improvement in the work or status of the individual. Many changes involve a mixture of positive and negative elements, and it is as important to stress the positive as it is to look for ways to ameliorate and not simply ignore the negative. This is not always possible. Some automation changes require major adaptation on the part of specific individuals if they are to survive in the newly created environment. Some changes downgrade existing jobs and it is important to determine whether or not the employee can be prepared for a different assignment, unless the person specifically prefers what is clearly understood to be a lower-level position. In automation some positions are upgraded, some are eliminated entirely, and that problem must be faced and discussed. Do not pretend or hope that individuals will not notice how changes have affected or promise (or threaten) to affect their work. They will notice, and without communication from management they will view the situation as far worse than it really is.

The Job Security Issue

Wilson Luquire's study of automation in academic libraries would undoubtedly find confirming counterpart reactions in other library settings.[2] Luquire found that the greatest concern in employees' reactions to automation was that of job security. People will dislike a system which they feel threatens their own jobs, and this only confirms Abraham Maslow's hierarchical ranking of needs. It is clear that anyone considering changing any subordinate's job, whether or not through automation, must deal with the employee's concern about job security.

The threat to job security is not an idle one. If backlogs can be eliminated through automation then it is indeed possible that existing personnel might be terminated. Alternatively, overtime payments might be halted, or the continued expansion of the group stopped or reversed through attrition. Any of these changes will be negatively perceived, and not unreasonably so.

If management has satisfactory and reassuring answers, these should obviously be volunteered before any questions are even asked. If there are no satisfactory answers, then management had better plan on how to deal with the dissatisfaction and resentment which is bound to follow. Individual and scattered resentment can be dealt with, and sometimes it may even be necessary to suppress it. However, the ability of large groups of employees to effectively undermine an unwelcome procedure will be much harder to cope with. If the group and its leaders do not accept the manager's premise because they see it as detrimental, the change will not work.

Resistance to Change

Automation represents change in the way things have been done. Change is threatening to most individuals, because no matter how unattractive the present may be, they have adapted to it. To some extent they have bent to meet the requirements of the job. To some extent they have bent the requirements of the job to meet their own preferences, with or without (usually without) the supervisor's knowledge and concurrence. The perceived virtue of any long-standing system is that people get used to it. It is because change represents an unknown and an uncontrollable new factor that individuals fear it and, in many cases, automatically and instinctively oppose it.

This fear of change is particularly prevalent in libraries. Until the advent of computerization, they had changed little in 100 years. The most recent major technological change in libraries before computers—typewriters—represented no threat to the system. To a great extent most libraries have been able to ignore the development of literature formats that did not meet their expectations by pretending that such materials did not belong in libraries. Automation cannot be ignored, although for a while some librarians tried to pretend that it did not apply to their operations. Not only does it address squarely some of the backlogs and staff shortages about which librarians have long complained, but it is championed by a new breed of professionals who have the attention of higher level management.

The Special Problems of Computers

Overly optimistic projections about the effects of computers have created special problems. A naive optimism of the early 1900s that technology would create a paradise on earth was echoed by the promises of computer technologists in the 1950s and 1960s. To some extent these exaggerated projections of how individuals will be changed by computer technology are still with us. They fail to take into account that while individuals are willing to make some adaptations to the specific characteristics of equipment, that willingness is limited. It has been noted by a number of recent critics that human beings are being asked to adapt to what makes machines efficient, rather than to have machines adapt to what makes people efficient. After the first wave of enthusiasm, resentment is inevitable.

In addition to objections to automation as an occasionally oversold concept, opposition can also be less rational. Many individuals see the computer as somehow dehumanizing. The glee with which newspapers announce a "computer error" in the mailing of tax statements, when inevitably the error was made by a human being, is an example of this attitude. Other examples come from such writers as Aldous Huxley (*Brave New World*), George

Orwell (*Nineteen Eighty-Four*) and Kurt Vonnegut (*Player Piano*), and filmmakers such as Charles Chaplin ("Modern Times") and Stanley Kubrick ("2001; A Space Odyssey"). These men sought to imbue technology with an evil genius of its own. Their works may be entertaining, but they are both exaggerated and unfair. More important, they propose no alternatives and no solutions.

The emotional negativism aroused by automation in any setting cannot be ignored. Rumors of incipient blindness and sterility caused by working at terminals have found no substantiation in any scientific tests, but that does not mean they will not have a significant impact on worker attitudes. Such charges must be anticipated, and they cannot be ignored.

As late as 1971 at least one prominent librarian was arguing, in an article humorously phrased but seriously intended, that no possible good could come out of any sort of automation of library operations.[3] It is the task of managers to make such critics see that technology is our servant and not our master.

Lessening Employees' Anxiety

Susan Baerg Epstein, in a brief article in *Library Journal,* has laid out clear planning guidelines to alleviate the morale problems that automating often brings.[4] What follows are some of her rules, with some elaboration:

1) Keep in mind the problems you are trying to address. How will automation potentially help? When faced with the challenge or danger of change, staff members frequently tend to forget that everything wasn't really so good in the "good old days."

2) Inform everyone from the start. Prospects of automation become the hottest topic of conversation, and a lack of facts will only lead to rumors. The facts may be a mixture of good and bad news; the rumors will all be bad.

3) Somebody has to be in charge. The Epstein article makes a point which this book will make repeatedly. Involving staff in the development process and drawing their suggestions (consultative management) is not the same thing as allowing the staff to actually

make decisions (consensus or democratic management). That works for some issues, but it certainly does not work in the area of automation. Decisions must be made by individuals with the responsibility and authority for making them. As Drucker has put it: "Involving workers in the management process is not the answer. It only corrupts good unionization." Epstein and Drucker are correct. Employees need to be listened to; they do not necessarily need a vote.

4) Involve everyone, particularly the critics. People other than managers may well have valid ideas. Even more important, though, is the fact that excluding people may produce antagonists. Individual workers have a passionate and understandable interest in changes that affect their work environment. In many cases their concerns once identified are easily incorporated in systems design. In other cases in which this is not possible, they must at least understand why it is not possible. Involve critics at this stage of discussion because it is far less dangerous than involving them later, because they have a right to be heard and because some of their criticisms might be valid.

5) Answer the concerns raised, to whatever extent possible. If answers are not possible, at least say so. Inevitably these concerns center primarily on issues of job security, on what is perceived as quality of the products produced, on style of individual work and independence of action, and on the future. Not all questions can be answered in detail, and not all the answers will be happily received. It is still better to provide some than to ignore the issues entirely. In this communications process, as in all others, the question "why" must be answered.

ADAPTING THE ORGANIZATIONAL STRUCTURE

The application of technology in libraries as in other organizations does affect organizational structure in a number of ways. Among these are an emphasis on centralization of decision making, a greater need for employees to accept managerial decisions, increased visibility of work of both inferior and superior employees and the manager's ability to accept solutions that are not always perfect.

The Pyramid of Organization

Most organizational structures are shaped like pyramids, with responsibility and authority focused on an ever-narrowing apex, and instructions flowing downward into a widening base. As noted by Drucker more than a decade ago, the pure and unrestricted use of the hierarchical relationships embodied in the pyramid is not well-suited to the systems decision concept required by technological implementation considerations. The systems decision concept cuts across organizational lines.

Drucker argues for a greater involvement of more individuals, but *not* for a decentralization of the decision process. If anything, automation involves a greater centralization of decisions. Somebody has to be in charge, although that individual would be well-advised to seek and evaluate advice from many sources. This point will be made again in this chapter and is worth stressing. The greater involvement of staff in consideration of automation is not the same thing as the delegation or abdication of the decision process to a committee or to a consensus. Some of the worst examples of automation projects without targets and without measurable results can be traced to an abdication of the decision process.

Changing How Managers Manage

The application of technology in the automation of libraries does indeed require discipline. Managers must get adherence to decisions without as much room as may be customary for individual acceptance or rejection of norms. Some writers argue that this dehumanizes the work process. Drucker, and I along with him, would disagree. The discipline of automation requires people to take a greater responsibility for their actions, for their correct decisions and their mistakes. Is this dehumanization, or is it really an elevation of the role and importance of the individual?

Much of the criticism of work at computer terminals centers on the fact that both qualitative and quantitative control are now possible. Individuals who do not work, or who do sloppy work, are now exposed. Yet, is this an undesirable quality? It is for those whose errors are now visible, but this visibility can be the basis of corrective criticism for which managers previously lacked tools.

The new visibility should also be of value to those workers whose superior performance is equally made visible. The fact that this is not generally considered an asset is because managers in libraries as in other work environments have failed to seize opportunities to praise and to reward superior performance. It is only because computer reporting is viewed as negative or at best neutral, and never as positive, that superior employees fail to perceive the opportunities in a system that can earn them deserved credit. There is a tendency to forget that superior employees are the ones about whose attitudes we should care most.

"GOOD ENOUGH" RATHER THAN "BEST"

There are a number of other general misconceptions about the implementation of technology. These have been very usefully identified in a *Harvard Business Review* article by Lowell Steele.[5] What Steele finds true for managers in general will certainly hold true for librarians, too. Among other things, Steele points out that managers often assume that the correct criterion for implementation of technological change is to find the best possible solution, and not merely one that is good enough. The result of this assumption is wasted time and effort. The search for perfection has both delayed and complicated many an automation process, and some have never gotten off the ground at all while the search for a still better solution continued. Steele also points out that the determination of what is a good solution is often not made through a series of careful and rational choices, but rather by convention. It is based on what people have come to expect or learned to expect.

Steele also argues that evolutionary advances are far preferable to major upheavals for most operational implementations. They involve less risk, are more timely and, on balance, are far more cost-effective than the selection of radically new technology. In short, these applications are "good enough," and library managers must never forget that the purpose of their automation, if indeed they automate, is not for its own sake but in order to improve or facilitate the meeting of one or more organizational objectives. It is when "elegant" systems, whose complexity exceeds the relatively mundane needs of the library, break down that sweeping indictments of all automation processes are most frequently heard.

Finally, in an argument which echoes both Drucker and other writers, Steele stresses that the implementation of technology requires the development of standards and procedures, the achievement of greater exactness and precision, and insistence on discipline and constraints.

REASONS FOR AUTOMATING

Automation is an essential consideration for all libraries, for a variety of reasons. First, it must be considered and evaluated (whether or not implemented), because libraries do not now function all that well under manual systems. They are underfunded, but more importantly they are understaffed, and when understaffing occurs, professionals work as clerks because clerical tasks predominate. Automation may change that mix. Second, it must be considered because there are many services that manually functioning libraries cannot provide at all, such as the cumulation of indexes, or the delivery of bibliographic or hard-copy information to remote locations. Third, libraries must consider automation because it provides the most direct and perhaps only realistic mechanisms for sharing bibliographic access and document availability, at a time when local holdings become increasingly inadequate. Finally, libraries must consider automation from the political standpoint. Automation represents change and innovation, and these are usually positively viewed by the outsiders who evaluate and judge us, and to whom we must appeal for funds and support. At the same time, considering automation does not require us to implement it for its own sake.

SUMMARY

In preparing for automation, the writings of Drucker, Luquire, Steele, Epstein and others should be consulted. In addition, the following guidelines should be kept in mind:

- As in any management decisions, the needs of the library are paramount. What are those needs? Can they be addressed without automation? How will automation solve these problems? Will it cause other problems in turn?

- Allow individual staff members enough time and information to adjust to the idea. Provide information, seek discussion and suggestions, allow for the needed education and training. In particular, address questions of how this change affects individuals—their work, their flexibility, and their potential for growth and advancement.

- To whatever extent possible, permit individuals to make the adaptation between the needs of the job and their own personal needs in their own way. Given half a chance, most of them will figure out a way to make the change personally tolerable. In the implementation of automation, some organizations fail to spell out needed criteria and ground rules. Many make more rules and in greater detail than needed. Allow subordinates as much flexibility and individuality as you can.

- Be firm with recalcitrants. It is one of the basic tenets of personnel administration that nothing works all the time. Enlightened practices of communication, education and training will probably satisfy the needs of the great majority of the employees affected, but there may still be a hard core of unreconstructed rebels whose opposition is emotional and whom no amount of reason will sway. Be prepared for this, and do not consider it a failure either of management style or of the automation process when it occurs. These individuals cannot be allowed to sabotage from within the implementation of change.

Management options in dealing with an employee opposing change obviously depend on the status of the employee and the needs of the library. It may be possible to transfer the individual to a post in which he or she is less affected by these changes and therefore not as prone to criticize them. That may be possible, but only if the individual is qualified for the new assignment, and if it represents a task which really needs to be done. Creating "busy work" is unfair to the library, to overworked staff members, and to the individual whose dignity has been insulted and whose time is being wasted. Little good comes of such temporizing transfers.

Ultimately, the individual who confronts the implementation of technological change despite his or her objections has but one set of alternatives. These two choices do not include staying behind to criticize and sabotage the process. They include, on the one hand, adaptation or acceptance and, on the other hand, quitting. Nobody should remain in a job or an organization whose priorities he or she finds personally offensive or humiliating. Resignation as a suggested alternative may seem harsh, but it is not. In some instances it is the kindest possible action.

NOTES

1. Drucker, Peter F., *Technology, Management and Society* (New York: Harper & Row, 1973).

2. Luquire, Wilson, "Attitudes Toward Automation/Innovation in Academic Libraries," *Journal of Academic Librarianship* 8 (January 1983):344-351.

3. Mason, Ellsworth, "The Great Gas Bubble Prick't; or Computers Revealed— By a Gentleman of Quality," *College and Research Libraries* 32 (May 1971): 181-196. Reactions to article, *College and Research Libraries* 32 (September 1971):384-392.

4. Epstein, Susan Baerg, "Implementation of an Automated System," *Library Journal* 108 (September 15, 1983):1771-1772.

5. Steele, Lowell, "Managers' Misconceptions About Technology," *Harvard Business Review* 61 (November-December 1983):133-140.

5

Leadership, Supervision and the Decision Process

As earlier chapters have discussed, the need to establish goals, articulate them through objectives and implement them through specific programs and strategies is essential for the success of any organization. It is particularly important for libraries, in which there is often a lack of solidly defined aims, and where there are no yardsticks with which to measure success or failure. Indeed, for many questions that arise in attempting to evaluate library service there are no objective, clear-cut answers. For example, when is it "reasonable" to expect a requested book to be in the collection and when is it not? What is a valid reference question, and when does a question represent an attempt to have someone else do work that should be personally accomplished? What is an acceptable cataloging backlog or delay in acquiring a requested item from interlibrary loan?

It is because specific criteria have seldom been established by either professional librarians or library users that expectations tend to be either unrealistically high or unnecessarily low. In neither case is there any particular commitment to the accomplishment of stated objectives, because they are recognized as approximations or as idealized states, and thus they can always be modified or extended as necessary. Such an approach is ineffective for the organization; even more important, it is also destructive to the will and morale of employees.

THE IMPORTANCE OF KNOWING THE RULES

As noted earlier, individuals like to play by rules, and they want to know what those rules are. While we like to win whatever games we play, we recognize that we cannot win all the time. What then becomes important is an understanding of what it takes to win, and a belief that with a given level of effort and involvement we can reap rewards.

Important games have referees who know the rules and see that they are administered fairly. In addition to wanting to know the rules, workers want to know what constitutes good or at least satisfactory performance. While they are willing to forgo criticism, they are not willing to forgo praise when they have done well. They also need to be able to have confidence in the fairness and capability of the referee—their manager. For the manager to inspire that confidence, he or she must have leadership qualities.

CHOOSING SUPERVISORS

Supervisors are supposed to be leaders, and the qualities that make a good leader are not necessarily the same as those that make a productive assembly line worker, typist or reference librarian. Laurence Peter has written in an amusing and yet very serious way about our societal insistence on promoting individuals for the wrong reasons.[1] We promote them because they have done well in their old jobs and not necessarily because we think they will do well in the next one. This is a serious concern for libraries at least as much as for other organizations, and it will receive more detailed treatment in Chapter 9.

For the moment, let us only consider Peter's claim that promotion, as a reward for capable performance, removes individuals from jobs they do well at and often places them in positions they cannot effectively handle. It is, he argues, a plan for incompetence, and we follow it because we view promotion as a reward, and perhaps the only reward that carries with it monetary recognition. To receive a substantial salary increase people must seek and accept promotion. The suggestion that hierarchical ranks need not automatically be tied to salary levels, and that subordinates can indeed be paid more than their bosses if their contribution is more valuable, has not penetrated most organizational policy-making. It certainly has had little impact on libraries.

When Supervisors Fail to Lead

Supervisors are supposed to be leaders and are given many advantages in assuming the leadership role. However, the assumption of that role is not automatic. Where supervisors fail to lead, others will step in to exercise this function.

Even in organizations in which there is a strong sense of purpose conveyed through management, leaders and followers will evolve. Indeed, in the most innocent of organizational dynamics, there is usually one individual who tends to decide for the group when to eat and where, what parties to plan and whom to invite. When this sort of leadership is comfortably accepted by other group members, management may even encourage the relationship. The wise supervisor in this sort of setting knows which individual must first be persuaded to accept a change in schedule or procedure.

Problems arise when supervisors are not leaders and when the real leaders subvert what the organization is trying to accomplish. The conflict is best illustrated in the classic confrontation between assembly line foremen and union shop stewards, both of whom compete for the attention and loyalty of the individual worker. The competition between union shop stewards who are leaders and foremen who may have been selected because of attributes such as seniority but who may not lead at all has proven so destructive in union/management communication that even unions have seen the management need to make changes. One very simple solution is the recognition that those who rise to leadership positions within a union are strong potential candidates for promotion to management.

While the conflicting values in libraries are never as sharp as in the confrontations described above, it is still necessary for us to understand the characteristics of a successful leader in a library environment so that we can look for these attributes in those whom we consider for promotion to management posts. It must be remembered that while leaders do indeed lead, they do not necessarily lead in what we consider the right direction.

Leadership Traits

What then are some of the characteristics of a successful leader? First of all, there is *intelligence*. Studies of leadership tend to show that a leader has somewhat greater intelligence than his or her followers. However, if the intelligence gap becomes too great then communication barriers begin to appear. A PhD research scientist is rarely an effective leader of library stack attendants.

A second attribute characteristic of leaders is *social sensitivity*. Leaders deal constantly with others and achieve their success largely through powers of persuasion. It is therefore important that they be able to sense and judge human reactions.

Leaders also share the characteristic of *active participation*. Since they initiate action for others, they are invariably alert, enthusiastic and interested in people. Individuals who are shy and retiring, who prefer solitude and resent the intrusion of others into their well-planned schedule, are not likely to be successful leaders.

Perhaps most important, leaders possess *communication skills*. They need not necessarily be silver-tongued orators, but they must be fluent and direct enough to be easily understood. Most leadership communication is informal and oral, and the ability to arouse interest through a concise verbal appeal is important.

If leadership qualities are what we should be seeking in the appointment of supervisors and managers, it is not difficult to understand why we so frequently fail in the appointment process, and why Laurence Peter leads us to the unhappy conclusion that frequently it is not the cream that rises to the top. It is particularly true in bureaucracies in which attributes of longevity, loyalty, unquestioned acceptance of higher instructions and an ability to stay out of controversy are the factors that qualify individuals for promotion. Unfortunately, avoiding controversy is often a result of an unwillingness to take stands and make decisions—the very things supervisors are supposed to do.

It is one of the assumptions of management theory that administrators prefer bright and aggressive subordinates who might have to be reined in or slowed down on occasion, but who are anxious to pull the organization forward by testing and extending the limits of their own authority. That assumption does not always hold true. Some, perhaps many or most, managers prefer the comfort of subordinates who always agree, who always do what they are told and who never put forward a new idea without first determining that it will be acceptable. Insecure managers may feel threatened by bright and articulate subordinates who might prove them to be wrong on occasion. By and large, managers get and retain the supervisors they prefer, most directly through promoting individuals they approve of. When an ambitious subordinate feels he or she is being kept too tightly reined by a defensive manager, that subordinate will seek other opportunities. When managers complain that their subordinates lack imagination and energy, it is usually because they have chosen such subordinates. At least, this is so if the manager made these appointments directly.

Sometimes the appointment of a new higher-level manager from the outside changes all the ground rules for subordinates. That change may involve a switch from an insistence on passivity to an encouragement of innovation. Sometimes it is the other way around. Management changes invariably have ripple effects throughout the organization. The organization chart may remain unaltered except in the names in each of the boxes, but that hierarchical structure does not even begin to suggest the fundamental changes which might have occurred.

When supervisors are also leaders there is a reasonably successful chance for effective management. In cases where the two roles are separate, trouble becomes a distinct possibility. The employees in an organization search for leadership, and if they do not find it in the appointed officials, they will seek it elsewhere.

SOURCES OF AUTHORITY

Supervisors and managers who have been officially designated differ from leaders who emerge through the natural selection process because they have authority. Authority can be defined as the legitimate right to direct or influence the behavior of others. That legitimacy, in turn, may derive from several sources.

Legality, Competence and Referent Power

Legality, or the inherent power of a given position, is the most obvious source of authority. It must be used sparingly and cautiously. The injunction "Do it because I told you to" is sometimes necessary, but it suggests that other and more appropriate sources of authority have failed. The subordinate is fully aware of the supervisor's right to order compliance, but that authority is then accepted resentfully and unwillingly.

If an opportunity exists to prove the supervisor wrong in issuing the order, the subordinate will find it. The use of legality as an instrument for securing compliance in libraries as in other organizations means that the more reasonable processes of communication have failed or that they have not been used at all. The supervisor who relies exclusively or primarily on legality has not only failed to explain but has also failed to enlist the commitment and enthusiasm of the subordinate in seeking a successful solution to the problem. In fact, the supervisor may have created an incentive for ensuring that the process fails.

There are far better and more effective sources for the exercise of authority than legality. One of these is a reliance on *competence*. Competence refers to personal knowledge, ability and skill. The acceptance of the competence of the decision maker is particularly important in professional groups. It is not necessary for the supervisor of data entry operations to be an excellent keyboarder, as long as that supervisor has an understanding of what is or is not reasonable as an expectation of performance. By contrast, instructions given to professional librarians by an individual whose competence they do not accept will lead to resentment. At a minimum, it then becomes important that the subordinates at least understand the supervisor's reasons for making the decision.

Referent power derives from acceptance of the authority figure as a role model. Most often this comes with experience and seniority, but in a library setting it can derive from election to professional society office, publication of a significant paper or participation on a committee.

Exercising Authority over Professional and Clerical Workers

Both competence and referent power as sources of authority are voluntarily ceded by the subordinate to the supervisor. They can never be demanded, and they are particularly significant in dealings among professionals. Therefore, particular care must be taken in the appointment of supervisors over groups of professionals to ensure that such individuals possess both the general qualifications for a successful manager and the professional respect of those whose work they will be supervising.

By contrast, the sources of authority in a production environment or in a clerical environment are far simpler to enumerate. They include the ability to reward and punish. Punishment involves withholding salary increases or promotions, demoting and firing, and also the more subtle actions of open criticism or avoidance. Unattractive as these alternatives are, they take on increasing importance in organizations in which one supervisor controls the work of many subordinates doing similar work.

Both professional and clerical staffs exist in libraries, particularly in large and complex libraries. Supervisory techniques used with bibliographic subject specialists are not necessarily the same as those employed with student stack attendants. While fairness, decency and compassion should underlie all supervisory action, the most effective supervisory techniques are those that are geared to the characteristics of the subordinate and not of the supervisor. Successful supervisors adapt their own principles and techniques to the individual and to the specific situation.

Charisma

A final characteristic of successful leaders, and therefore a very appropriate consideration in the search for effective supervisors, is *charisma*. Charismatic leaders demand loyalty and obedience, but find that these responses are willingly given. Charismatic leadership can of course result in disastrous excesses. Even in office settings the use of a supervisor's charismatic powers to develop a cult of personality can serve to undermine the objectives of the larger organization. Nevertheless, the use of charisma as a management technique should not be underestimated.

Charisma represents the highest of the three levels of persuasion available to the supervisor. The lowest, and least effective, is that of raw power, force and coercion. The second, and probably most socially acceptable, is that of explanation and discussion. This method seeks voluntary compliance, and where that can be achieved it is the most successful form of involvement. The highest level and most direct technique for securing cooperation is the charismatic approach. Where it works, it works superbly.

The most obvious drawback of the charismatic approach is that it is based on personality rather than on reason, and it does not transfer from one supervisor to the next. The new manager who succeeds a charismatic supervisor without having the same amount of charisma faces a difficult problem. He or she inherits a situation which produced successful results without the tools to continue that same process. For all these reasons, we fall back on explanation and discussion as the most fundamentally effective supervision techniques, particularly in a professional environment. However, one caution must be sounded. Failure to achieve a high level of subordinate cooperation cannot be used as an excuse for failing to find a way to make sure that necessary work gets done. Ultimately, successful supervisors are pragmatists. They do what works. If one method fails, another must be sought. (Chapter 6 will deal further with techniques and excesses involved in seeking voluntary compliance.)

THE COURAGE TO DECIDE

The fundamental responsibility of the supervisor and manager (and these terms are usually indicative only of levels of status and not of a difference in basis of authority) is the making of decisions. These decisions are expected to facilitate the process of accomplishing the objectives of the unit and of the larger organization. Even in the most straightforward of operations, problems arise. Supervisors are needed to resolve these conflicts—correctly if possible, but even incorrectly if necessary. In most cases even a bad decision is preferable to no decision, because the work environment cannot endure delay and individuals feel uncomfortable with uncertainty.

Why People Avoid Decision Making

Decision making is fundamental to management, but some managers go to extraordinary lengths to avoid it. Part of the reason may come from inherent indecisiveness—what one well-known comic strip character calls being wishy-washy. Individuals who exhibit continual indecisiveness are incapable of being good supervisors. The courage to make decisions is not a trait that can be learned but one that must be an integral part of the supervisor's personality.

Some poor managers are simply afraid of the possibility of making bad decisions. Good decisions obviously are preferable to poor ones, but the overwhelming fear of making poor decisions can be paralyzing. Individuals so afflicted cannot be managers. Any good manager has made some bad decisions. What makes a manager good is that he or she also has made many good decisions and has learned from the bad ones.

A third group of individuals who avoid decision making are those who are perfectionists. Managers hope to make good decisions, and good decisions usually require information. However, all possible information is rarely at hand when a decision must be made. The manager who insists that no decision can be made until all possible factors have been considered may end up making no decision at all.

Signs of Decision Avoidance

Because managerial appointments in libraries as elsewhere are frequently made without consideration of the candidate's willingness and psychological ability to make decisions, decision avoidance has become a highly developed and costly work practice. Because it is employed so widely, it is useful to identify some of its techniques and characteristics. If all else fails, the individual who has fallen prey to an "avoid decisions at all costs" type of manager will at least recognize what is being done. Decision avoidance is found in all types of organizations and is frequently characteristic of library managers. The paralysis which can result from this tactic is often even more damaging than what occurs when managers make decisions without enough information.

Concern is raised in some of the library management literature about willful and autocratic managers who force their decisions on others, and there are undoubtedly examples of this type. However, they are relatively rare. There are far more cases in libraries of managers who refuse to decide at all.

Supervisors who want to avoid making decisions get very good at it. They find ways to place blame so that the avoidance does not appear to be their fault. Means of doing this include:

• Inaction: Obviously, the supervisor who has not had time to read a proposal or memorandum cannot be expected to respond to it. Most of the time the plea of being too busy is a sham. People find time to do the things they consider important. If communications are not being read, it is because the individuals to whom they are addressed do not want to read them. In any case, being too busy is not an acceptable excuse. If supervisors are too busy to read correspondence, they must take up this problem with the next higher level of management, because either the workload or a lack of organization is preventing them from doing their job. When inaction is used as a conscious decision-avoidance tactic, the subordinate is put in a completely intolerable position.

• Invisibility: In a sense, invisibility is a variant of inaction. Doors are always closed, meetings are postponed or canceled, telephone calls are never returned. Again, if the supervisor is really too busy, then it is up to him or her to do something about it. However, if this is only a tactic to avoid dealing with a problem, that tactic will become quickly apparent. Subordinates will become angry and perhaps ultimately lethargic.

• Creation of impenetrable obstacles: This is probably the nastiest of all decision-avoidance techniques, both because it creates a pretense of activity and support and because it causes useless additional work for the subordinate. This tactic is usually expressed as "Yes, but. . ." The "but" invariably involves the need to seek further information, to coordinate with others and to reach agreement with others who are not even remotely involved. All this takes time and gives the decision avoider respite while being able to claim support and encouragement. When the subordinate finally becomes discouraged and gives up, the manager can quite piously claim regret, since he or she was "quite supportive." As noted, it is a vicious game played all too frequently, and there is probably no action more rapidly destructive of morale and initiative. This is not to imply that ideas and suggestions need not be coordinated or that further information is never needed. It is only when these barriers are artificially erected to avoid doing what the manager is supposed to do—make decisions—that the process becomes destructive.

• Negation: Supervisors who automatically reject all new ideas are a bit easier to understand, but it is important for the subordinate to have some idea of why all initiatives are rejected. It may be that what is occurring is the rather natural (at least for most people) fear and distrust of the new and different. When negation takes place for this reason, rather than simply as a tactic for decision avoidance, there are ways to improve the situation. The most obvious and direct is an informal verbal presentation of the idea, in a casual and non-threatening setting. Sometimes several repetitions are required to remove the threat of newness. This approach clearly will not work with inactive or invisible managers, because such individuals will not give their subordinates the time needed to present their ideas. Negation-prone managers who are inclined to reject innovation will certainly find both the time and reasons for doing so.

• Passing the Buck: Managers who insist that all decisions must be made at a higher level do not perform a very useful function, and this quickly becomes apparent to their subordinates. Individuals who insist that someone in higher authority must decide frequently fail to seek that decision, thereby dooming the idea to total obscurity.

• Abdication: Abdication is a process that may indeed lead to a decision, but it will not be a decision in which the manager shared, and the presumed expertise that caused his or her appointment to a management post is totally wasted. Abdication is usually made to a committee. This tactic appears safe because group decisions usually protect the participants in case the decision is wrong. Abdication to a group decision process carries with it the further attraction of at least appearing to be democratic or participatory, both of which are often considered to be virtues in management. For some issues, abdication to a democratic process is desirable. For others, a consultative approach to seek input for the manager's own decision is appropriate. In some situations, consultation is inappropriate, and the manager must simply make the decisions and take the risks.

No matter which approach to decision avoidance is employed, no good can come of it. Unfortunately, as we have already seen, for libraries in particular the prevalence of managers who are not trained to manage makes decision avoidance an all-too-common phenomenon. Organizational dynamics demand decisions. While good decisions are obviously preferable to poor ones, in many situations any decision—which then allows everyone to adapt and go on from there—is preferable to no decision at all.

NOTES

1. Peter, Laurence J., *The Peter Principle* (New York: William Morrow, 1969).

6

Approaches to Decision Making

The primary responsibility of the manager is to reach decisions or at least to see that decisions are reached. The preceding chapter discussed, among other things, how some managers try to avoid decision making. This chapter will describe and evaluate how decisions are in fact made.

DECISION-MAKING STYLES

There are five basic methods managers use to reach decisions. Some managers use a combination of these approaches.

1) Solving all problems directly, using (or ignoring) whatever information is at hand. Individuals who employ this approach do not share problems with anyone, nor do they consult anyone prior to reaching a decision. Their decisions usually appear to be bolts from the blue; in many cases subordinates did not even know there was a decision to be reached.

2) Deciding before reaching a decision what information to obtain from subordinates. The purpose of the information request may not be explained, and the subordinates who supply the requested information usually do not know why they have been asked. Their supervisor has defined their role as providing information, not as generating or evaluating alternative solutions.

3) Sharing the problem, or at least part of the problem, with individual subordinates on a one-to-one basis. The process of

determining which individuals are to be consulted may be based on a perception of each person's ability to contribute, or it may be based on the manager's desire to obtain friendly and encouraging support for general directions already established. When the manager makes the decision, it may or may not reflect the influence of the subordinate.

4) Sharing the problem with subordinates as a group, thereby obtaining ideas and suggestions, collectively as well as individually. These ideas and suggestions are then freely discussed by the group as a whole. After the interchange, the manager makes a decision, which may or may not reflect a consensus or majority opinion. This style is generally known as consultative management.

5) Sharing the problem with subordinates as a group to evaluate alternatives and to seek consensus. In this case, the manager acts more like a chairman or presiding parliamentary officer than a leader, and makes no attempt to influence the group toward his or her own solution. The manager also makes a commitment in advance to accept and implement any solution which has the support of the group. In some situations the manager absents himself or herself from the discussion entirely to avoid even appearing to exert influence. This style is generally known as participatory or democratic management.

Decision-Making Methods Generally to Be Avoided

The first three styles examined above are generally unacceptable, in part because they fail to take into account the need of individual employees to understand if not share in what is going on, and to understand their own importance to this process. These decision-making styles are also unacceptable because they are almost guaranteed to ensure bad decisions, in addition to a disinterested or alienated staff.
The first style assumes that the manager possesses a wealth of information and knowledge not usually available to one individual within a large organization. Decisions reached in this

solitary manner will indeed be reached rapidly, but they will often be wrong simply because they will be made with ignorance of important or even crucial factors. In addition, as mentioned earlier in this book, subordinates who have had no voice in the decision feel no responsibility for seeing that it succeeds. In fact, they may well feel a perverse pleasure at seeing the tactic fail.

The second style is only slightly more open. While the manager is seeking information, he or she is seeking it from selected sources, often to get information that will support a decision already reached. Beyond this, librarians know quite well from their own question negotiation training that an improperly phrased question from a reference client will often yield an answer that is correct for the question but not for the problem. The question "Who is your best reference librarian?" will probably produce an answer, but that answer will not be as useful as the one which poses the real problem: "There is going to be an assistant branch supervisor vacancy soon which requires a heavy concentration on reference work. Do you feel any of your subordinates are worthy of consideration for this promotion?"

The third style permits more involvement than the first two, but still causes some problems. Sharing the problem with some subordinates leads to a feeling of exclusion on the part of those who were not asked. Moreover, as to those subordinates who were consulted, people whose advice is sought do not necessarily expect that their suggestions will always be followed, but they do expect to be told *why* their suggestion was not acted on. This is a reasonable expectation. One of the greatest alienating effects of implementing the style but not the substance of participatory or democratic management is the perception that advice was sought and then ignored. The individuals involved feel more alienated than if they had never been asked in the first place, and they are likely to decide never to put themselves in a similar position again.

This is not to suggest that the above three styles, and particularly the third, are never appropriate. Managers may be faced with delicate and sensitive issues which cannot be shared directly with subordinates because the subordinates are the subject of the concern. For example, it may be appropriate in certain settings to share criteria for salary determinations or for layoffs but not the specific implementation of those criteria.

In general, however, there is clearly more secrecy and mystique in the management process than is warranted. Although there are some individuals who prefer to operate in such an environment, most managers do not. Secrecy is most likely to occur when the manager has no confidence in the judgment of subordinates, or believes that subordinates are not really interested in participating, especially when difficult and painful decisions are involved. This belief, however, is very inaccurate. Subordinates are usually well aware that problems exist, and sometimes they view these even more pessimistically than management. They also realize that resources are finite and that the power of the manager is limited. They can accept bad news, and they can accept criticism if it is not presented in a destructive or humiliating form.

What subordinates seek is some assurance that their own concerns are at least being considered, that decisions are being reached equitably and that these decisions can be implemented productively. At a minimum, this assurance is dependent on rapid and open communication of decisions, together with an explanation of how these will be implemented. Beyond this, employees require an explanation of why these decisions were reached. As noted earlier in this book, all workers need to know reasons, and this is particularly true of professional workers. As will be stressed in the following section, it is not necessary that subordinates agree with the manager's decision, although obviously that is helpful. It is important that they understand why the decision makes sense to its maker and that it was not made arbitrarily, capriciously or malevolently.

Appropriate Decision-Making Approaches

It is not impossible to provide these assurances when using the first three decision styles, but the fourth and fifth—the consultative and the participatory (democratic) styles—are far more appropriate when they can be implemented. Each is appropriate in specific settings.

In general, the participatory process should be used when possible. However, according to my observations, the participatory process or at least the *semblance* of a participatory process has been overused in libraries. In part this is because librarian peer groups and writers of management literature have often insisted that participation is the best management style in all settings. That statement, like most management generalizations, is nonsense. Overuse of the participatory process has also occurred because, as already noted, many librarians are at heart opposed to any management structure. They embrace participation because it fits their view of society, and they feel comfortable with it.

When participative or democratic structures are used improperly, however, they can lead to bad decisions, as can any process. They can also lead to an unconscionable delay in reaching any decision, because the consensus process is often slow. Worst of all, they can lead to total alienation when the decisions they yield are rejected by higher authority as unrealistic or irrelevant.

MAKING DECISIONS EFFECTIVELY IN LIBRARIES

A number of factors determine which approach works best for making decisions in specific library situations. No matter which option is selected for dealing with a given question—i.e., the consultative style or the participatory process—the manager must equip his staff with whatever data they need to arrive at conclusions.

Setting Limits on the Range of Possible Decisions

In the consultative and democratic decision processes, it is first necessary to determine what range of solutions is acceptable. That determination must be conveyed to the participants under either of these two formats to avoid misleading them. For example, a solution that requires a doubling of the staff or a 50% increase in salaries may be attractive and easily decided upon, but if there is no hope of implementing it, then the process becomes destructive. If the question concerns ways to increase the output of the cataloging department, then the supervisor must explain immediately whether or not the addition of staff is a possibility. In the absence of such a guideline, the manager can be certain that the response, in either a consultative or a participatory decision environment, will call for more employees. If the group is told in advance that this is out of the question, much time and alienation can be avoided. Furthermore, the supervisor should avoid the temptation to find a scapegoat by agreeing that such solutions would be nice if only higher management were more reasonable. As noted by Hedberg[1], the suggestion that the problem be solved by having everyone work harder is also not worthwhile. It may indeed be possible for everyone to work harder, but staff will not accept such a self-indictment of prior indolence.

In both the use of the consultative and the participatory processes, it is the manager's responsibility to communicate to the group what can and cannot be considered in making a given decision. In some instances the range of satisfactory responses can be quite open-ended where few restrictions are imposed. For example, any schedule for the library picnic may be acceptable that does not interfere with normal hours of operation. Other rules may need to be far more restrictive. For example, it may be that no solution that requires spending more money or hiring more staff members can be considered. In other instances, organizational or legal restrictions may cover reassignments or promotions. Announcing the rules may cause irritation, but nobody ever suggested that management was a popularity contest. The alternative of allowing staff members to make recommendations or even decisions (in the democratic participatory process) that turn out to be unacceptable is far worse.

The Case for Consultative Management

For all the reasons enumerated above, and because libraries operate with very limited resources and rather limited decision options, consultative management is usually a better procedure to follow for major issues in libraries than participatory management. This approach is not necessarily viewed negatively by staff members. As noted earlier, not everyone wants to share the responsibility of making decisions. However, everyone appreciates knowing what is and what is not permissible. A consultative system in which advice and opinions are openly solicited, acknowledged and considered can help develop both morale and staff involvement.

One requirement of consultative management techniques must be kept in mind at all times, and especially when preferred advice is not being accepted. That requirement is telling subordinates *why* particular decisions are made. Often two individuals will offer contradictory recommendations. The manager must explain why one person's advice was taken (if it was) and why the other's advice was rejected. These explanations do not have to convince the employee of the correctness of the decision, although it is obviously preferable when this occurs. All that is required, though, is to explain that the decision was rational. For a subordinate to respond, "I understand why you decided as you did, but I still think you are wrong," is probably a satisfactory ending to the discussion.

When Is the Participative Process Preferable?

Managers should leave to the participative or democratic process issues for which a range of responses is satisfactory. This includes topics on which the manager may indeed have an opinion, but for which that opinion is neither significant nor necessarily better informed. It has already been noted that managers must learn to differentiate between what is important and what is not, and therefore between issues for which their own preference is or is not particularly significant. The less important issues may not be crucial to the main effort of the library, but they may still arouse a considerable amount of strong feeling.

For example, methods for determining vacation scheduling do not matter to the supervisor nearly as much as the assurance that there is a method, that it is clearly understood, and that it assures adequate staffing at all times. As another example, in an academic library one group of librarians may opt for faculty status, with the attendant benefits including tenure and the attendant danger of having to meet faculty standards for scholarly productivity. Another group in the same library may prefer a separate librarian status, with lower prestige and benefits but also lower risks. Such a dual-status setup may be perfectly satisfactory, as long as each participant understands the pros and cons of the arrangement for which he or she has opted. The situation is somewhat similar to one which arises in performance evaluations, an issue that will be discussed in Chapter 9.

Asking the Right Question

Finding viable solutions through either the consultative or the participatory management process depends on framing the question properly. The question "How can we catalog more?" is probably too open-ended. However, "How do we catalog more without increasing staff or overtime and without working harder (because it is a given that we are all working as hard as we can)?" might produce some useful answers. It might even be desirable to add the further caveats "and without decreasing quality or increasing backlogs."

When focused on the proper question, the group might identify approaches acceptable both to itself and to management. Acceptability to both groups is important; a staff that does not accept the workability of a decision will see to it that it fails, and a solution unacceptable to management is no solution at all. It is probable that a satisfactory decision can be found, but there is no assurance. Not all problems have satisfactory solutions, and managers have to get used to that. What will sometimes be required is to go back to the drawing board and redefine the problem, but managers should not do this unless it is really necessary.

ORBITAL DECISION MAKING

Brief mention must be made of another form of decision structuring that occurs within organizations. The term "orbital" has recently come into vogue to describe decision structures which are largely participative, but in which a body of representatives from each work group (rather than the entire staff) makes the decisions. That body can either be appointed by management or elected by employees, although the whole framework of democratic participation would argue for election, to avoid the appearance of just another form of devious management control.

The orbital management concept has had some application in libraries, and some description in the literature[3]. For a large library staff in particular, the search for consensus among 75 or 100 people might take more time than even the most patient administrator could endure. It is for this reason that representatives are selected.

Managers referring problems to an orbital decision group must still make clear whether or not the group is free to reach any decision, to reach decisions within certain parameters, or just to advise but not decide. The manager who overrules a democratically reached decision by a body that has been given every reason to consider its role more than advisory is asking for trouble. He or she will not only alienate the members but will also strain the process of participation in any form.

DELEGATION

Up to now we have been discussing techniques for involving subordinates as a group in the decision process. There is, of course, another possibility—permitting decision making by an individual subordinate. That process is called delegation. The management literature is full of articles dealing with this topic. Delegation is a good thing, all of these writers argue, and we should be doing more of it. Nobody is opposed to delegation. At the same time, however, there is also general agreement that it does not work nearly as well as it should. Three basic books on delegation can be recommended for further reading. The first, by Laird and Laird[4], is probably the most fundamentally complete, but the reader is warned that it is somewhat dated and that the writing style is sexist. The other two, by Valentine[5] and Steinmetz[6], provide useful insights in a more contemporary setting.

It is important to differentiate between delegation and the participatory group techniques described earlier in this chapter. Delegation *appears* democratic because the manager shares decision making. It is not truly democratic, because the individual who holds the delegated authority may turn out to be autocratic and is, in effect, the sole decision maker, i.e., the group is not consulted.

Delegation differs from work assignment. In the latter, tasks are assigned and their performance may lead to the identification of problems, but the manager reserves to himself or herself the right to make all decisions. (Work assignments may also involve situations in which decisions are made by an orbital or participatory structure.) In work assignment, tasks but no authority are transferred. Such an approach is not delegation.

Authority, Responsibility and Accountability

Delegation involves giving a subordinate both the authority and the responsibility for a task for which the subordinate is then held accountable. There are three key words in that sentence. *Authority* in good part entails having the resources (people, materials, dollars) necessary to carry out the delegated task. Such authority must be transferred publicly, so that all those concerned know about it. It does little good to inform employee A that he or she has the authority to assign work to employee B, if employee B has not been told. That may seem obvious, but it is a common failing of the delegation process. *Responsibility* means that the individual must see to it that whatever tasks are to be carried out are actually accomplished. Finally, *accountability* involves accepting both the rewards and the punishment that accompany success or failure.

Delegation differs quite markedly from the democratic, or participatory, decision process, in which authority can indeed be transferred but responsibility becomes diffused. In the event a bad decision is made, it is difficult to blame an entire staff or a committee of a dozen, and it is impossible to punish them. Those who would misuse the participatory process see this quite clearly. Thus, the inability to assign responsibility and accountability in a democratic decision-making structure sometimes works to the disadvantage of those who seek reward levels based on the merit of performance. In general, delegation to a committee makes sense only if the problem is so complex that diverse contributions are required.

Just as delegation differs from work assignment, it also differs from total abdication of responsibility. In delegation, objectives and the available resources, including time, are still identified by the manager.

Delegation, as opposed to promotion, is finite. Once the goal is accomplished, the subordinate relinquishes authority, responsibility and accountability.

Delegation is difficult for many supervisors not only because of a common reluctance to give up authority, but also because delegation, unlike assignment of tasks, spells out results to be achieved but not the approach to be used. It measures accomplishment and not method, and it is difficult for many supervisors to resist dabbling or at least offering "helpful" suggestions. Although it is one of the givens of management theory that enough authority must be provided to match the responsibility assigned, in practice this rarely occurs. One reason for this is that "authority" is considered a dirty word in management terminology, because it implies despotism and a lack of freedom. Managers often prefer to deal in generalities, asking others to cooperate without any clear understanding of what happens if they do not. "Responsibility," on the other hand, is a clean word in management parlance. As a result, responsibility is usually spelled out fairly clearly, while authority is primarily spelled out in the negative, stressing what may not be done rather than what may.

Individuals who lack enough explicit authority to carry out their responsibilities make use of two methods to broaden the scope of their authority. The first of these, implied authority, would not be necessary at all if authority were spelled out more clearly. It relies ultimately on the common sense argument that if one is going to be responsible for accomplishing something, then it is obvious that certain authority is required, even if not spelled out. Use of implied authority depends on the premise that everyone in an organization desires to appear reasonable, and will try to avoid the appearance of being arbitrary or negative.

The second source of additional authority, acquired authority, is more difficult to defend. It is usually sought without the manager's approval or even knowledge. Acquired authority includes rights developed through negotiation with others in the organization, and those simply assumed in the process of filling a vacuum. If a decision must be made and the boss is not around to make it, the principle of acquired authority suggests that the subordinate makes a needed decision even if technically it is outside his or her narrowly defined scope of authority. Here again the principle of appearing reasonable comes into play. Finally, acquired authority includes the ability to eliminate unproductive or unnecessary work. It is likely that nobody will even notice, but even if they do they will find it difficult to insist that needless work should have been performed.

Weaknesses of the Delegation Process

The reader will see quickly why the delegation process does not work very well, despite an almost total commitment to its use at least in principle. Some managers find the process of delegation painful and unnatural. They have fought hard to acquire authority and power, and they are reluctant to give it away. They may distrust the motives of their subordinates or, more likely, doubt their abilities to carry out the complexities of a delegated task. Subordinates themselves may be reluctant to receive delegated assignments, perhaps because they doubt their own abilities, because they do not enjoy the need to stake out implied or acquired authority, or because they seek to avoid risk. The acceptance of direct delegation does indeed carry risk for both parties.

Comparison with Other Techniques

Despite all these concerns and caveats, management experts are nearly unanimous in their insistence that delegation is a healthy process and one that should be more frequently employed. In the absence of delegation all authority remains centralized, all knowledge and all reasons for making decisions remain for the most part uncommunicated, and all of the alienations common to autocratic organizations set in.

Participatory management can solve some of these problems, but it can not ensure good decisions and it has no way to punish bad ones. Since no criteria are normally established, it is even difficult to determine what represents a good or at least an acceptable decision.

Consultative management retains this control, but also incorporates a drawback in the decision process: the finite ability of the manager to absorb ever-increasing workloads. In the consultative as well as the autocratic model, all decisions stop in the absence of a manager or a specifically named alternate.

Delegation involves the appointment of "little managers" for temporary and finite assignments. This provides the manager some basis for evaluation of subordinates. Properly performed, the process will reward those who are worthy of reward, punish, or at least fail to reward, incompetents or those unwilling to accept authority, and point the way to future promotions in an open and highly visible environment in which everyone can see both the process and the rationale. As already noted, the ability to distinguish and reward quality performance, and to do so in an open manner, is essential for the success of any organization. Egalitarianism—a process in which everyone is treated exactly the same regardless of performance—is an ineffective management method because the noncompetitive environment this creates is one in which poor performers will thrive while strong performers will leave to find a place where their assets are appreciated. Managers must fight for systems of performance reward and punishment.

Delegation carries risk, but this risk is necessary and is frequently not as great as initially perceived. In many cases, subordinates can indeed do more than managers think them capable of, provided that the delegation is full and open, and provided that success is supported. It is also essential that managers choose the right people for the process. Sometimes subordinates must be persuaded to accept more authority and responsibility. Subordinates should never be forced to do so, just as they should never be forced to accept promotion against their own better judgment. Both processes are almost guaranteed to fail.

NOTES

1. Hedberg, Bo, et al., "Camping on Seesaws. Prescriptions for a Self-Designing Organization," *Administrative Sciences Quarterly* 21(1)(1976):41-65.

2. Parkinson, C. Northcote, *Parkinson's Law and Other Studies in Administration* (Boston: Houghton-Mifflin, 1957).

3. Howard, Edward N., "The Orbital Organization," *Library Journal* 95 (May 1, 1970):1712-1715.

4. Laird, Donald A., and Laird, Eleanor C., *The Technique of Delegation* (New York: McGraw-Hill, 1957).

5. Valentine, Raymond F., *Initiative and Managerial Power* (New York: AMACOM, 1973).

6. Steinmetz, Lawrence L., *The Art and Skill of Delegation* (New York: Addison-Wesley, 1976).

7

Employee Recruitment and Selection

It appears obvious that the process of recruitment and selection must follow the identification and description of the position to be filled, and yet that step is sometimes not taken. Libraries are among the organizations for which sharp and sometimes unbridgeable distinctions usually exist between professional and clerical employees. In such a setting the first task of the recruitment process is to identify the kind of need that exists and the requirements a prospective employee must therefore satisfy. That relationship is not as simple as it might appear.

DEFINING JOBS FOR RECRUITMENT PURPOSES

Organizational goals, objectives, strategies and programs lead to the definition of specific tasks, and these in turn lead to the determination of what jobs exist that need to be filled. In the hiring and selection process it is important to know what those jobs are and what they require. Work consists of a series of responsibilities and tasks that need to be performed, and these are assigned to various individuals. Newly evolving concepts of job rotation, job enrichment and job sharing make the process of job definition somewhat more complex but do not in any way eliminate its need. It is still necessary to know who is going to be doing what, when and to what standards.

In the hiring process managers should be looking for people to fit tasks and not adapting tasks to what people would like or are able to do. When this latter phenomenon occurs, and it occurs all too frequently, the organization loses its sense of direction and purpose. Individuals permitted to do what they enjoy without regard to its relevance soon lose the sense of contribution to the accomplishment of overall objectives which is so important. Fitting jobs to people requires a complete restructuring of plans every time there is a staff change. Quite rapidly everyone becomes aware that there really are no plans, or that plans are simply statements of convenience that reflect what is going to happen anyway. When that occurs, libraries like other operational units lose their drive for accomplishment.

OVERQUALIFIED EMPLOYEES

Most organizations, and libraries in particular, lean toward overqualification in the hiring process—that is, they hire more professionals and fewer clerks than task assignments might warrant. There are several reasons for this. One is that the use of more professionals conveys a higher level of prestige to the supervisor, and that rationale also applies to the selection of higher- rather than lower-level professionals. Having a subordinate staff of Ph.D.s reflects favorably on the organization and the supervisor. It is also argued that professionals provide more flexibility to an organization than clerks, in that professionals are assumed to be able to perform clerical duties more easily than clerks can be assigned professional tasks. In fact, this may be assumed to be improper even if plausible. Finally, some managers will argue that since professionals are more difficult to recruit and to justify, and since they have a lower turnover rate, it is wise to hire not only the greatest number of professionals allowed, but also the most highly qualified ones that can be found.

Thus, it is not uncommon, particularly in academic libraries but also in others, to find degreed librarians filling clerical posts with little if any hope of future advancement. It is even more common in academic libraries to find senior professionals in junior positions, sometimes but not always at junior salaries. It is also a frequent practice to select candidates with advanced degrees and many years of professional experience for positions that really require neither. For some major academic libraries it is literally impossible for candidates without experience to acquire even the lowliest of professional positions. The presumption is that they should acquire experience elsewhere and then apply. Since all professional organizations, and particularly large ones, have low-level work to be done at the professional level, the tactic makes little sense.

Problems Associated with Overqualified Employees

The tendency to fill the roster with overqualified individuals does have some attractions, but these are far out numbered and outweighed by the pitfalls. The discussion of job descriptions in Chapter 9 makes the point that evaluation of employees must be based on accomplishments related to the job to be performed. Similarly, the selection of candidates should also be directly related to the job to be performed and the skills and qualifications it requires. In all probability, status and salary are already tied to that standard.

The stockpiling of overqualified individuals for jobs well below their capabilities usually causes problems of morale and ultimately performance, even if the candidates accept the positions willingly. Most immediately, they do not fit the pattern of the work force of which they are a part. They are either paid too much for the work they are performing, which causes resentment among those performing similar work at lower pay, or they are paid salaries in line with the work being performed, but well below what they would receive if they could obtain work suited to their capabilities. This can cause alienation and have a negative effect on enthusiasm and loyalty. Nobody can really expect file clerks with masters degrees to stay any longer than they absolutely have to, and while some individuals accept their fate willingly or at least stoically, others show their unhappiness on almost a daily basis.

While organizational hiring rules do not normally permit overqualified individuals to be discriminated against, they do not require that they be favored either. In other words, unnecessary experience for a job that requires none, or advanced degrees for positions for which these are not specified, can be and probably should be considered irrelevant.

The criterion used by the author when approaching his university personnel department about the need to fill a nonprofessional position is to specify both skills and job attitude required. The statement "I want a secretary who not only possesses strong secretarial skills, but who thinks being a secretary is an important and meaningful job" is an example of the most effective kind of communication between a manager with a vacancy and those who interview and hire.

Dealing with Overqualified Employees

If overqualified individuals are hired on the premise that they are being stockpiled, then the library must develop both plans and criteria to make upward mobility possible. Assuming that they perform satisfactorily, will such individuals be given special consideration for promotion? If these employees perform well, they should indeed have an advantage over outside candidates about whom little is known and about whom, as we shall note, very little of substance can be learned. On the other hand, if internal candidates perform poorly, then they are already disqualified from promotional opportunities.

If the library does make a general practice of employing overqualified candidates, then, at the very minimum, opportunities and expectations for advancement must be discussed with them, realistically and frequently. They may stay even if there are no chances for advancement, either by preference or because of lack of choices. At least they will know what they can and cannot expect. The need for more communication, and its general paucity in libraries as in other organizations, is a recurring problem.

PROMOTING FROM WITHIN

As already noted, the comparison of internal and external candidates is rarely evenhanded. In many cases enough is known about an internal candidate to ascertain that he or she should receive the promotion. There is nothing wrong with this. Unfortunately, in a mockery of fair play, external applicants are sometimes lured into a competition in which they have no realistic chance. As a teacher of library school students, this writer urges them to inquire as to whether the positions for which they are interviewing also have internal candidates and how the determination will be made. Comparison of both types of applicants can rarely be equitable.

In general, organizations prefer to promote from within. Doing so is wise if they can avoid diluting the quality of either the search or the position description. Internal candidates represent a known quantity. The organization already knows about their experience, their education and their intelligence. More important, managers have observed their attitude, their dependability and their ability to get along with others. If all of these traits are positive, selecting internally presents far less of a risk; as we will note, risk avoidance is key to personnel selection, particularly for junior positions.

Selecting internal candidates also has several other advantages. It avoids the cost and time of relocation, and it creates a positive and hopeful atmosphere within the organization. Employees who see others being promoted may feel encouraged, particularly those who aspire to growth and promotion.

At the same time, too much of any good thing can be dangerous. Promotions from within tend to limit the organization to familiar attitudes and ideas. While this is helpful in avoiding friction, it also shields the library from the freshness of new ideas and new approaches. It is perfectly natural for both individuals and organizations to assume that they already know everything worth knowing and that unfamiliar approaches are not worth considering. Outspoken outsiders can cause some resentment because they ask questions and challenge values and decisions long established. However, that process of reevaluation and revalidation is a healthy and necessary one.

HIRING FROM OUTSIDE

When no suitable candidate is available within an organization, it becomes necessary to hire an outsider. This process can cause resentment on the part of the existing staff. Dealing with this resentment and finding a well-qualified new employee are tasks which require great care.

Avoiding Mistakes

The evaluation of outside candidates is very much a defensive process, particularly for junior positions. The primary emphasis is not on finding the one best candidate, although that would certainly be desirable. Rather, it is on avoiding the hiring of an inappropriate applicant.

There are several reasons for this. First of all, most entry-level professional positions in libraries can be performed satisfactorily by perhaps half the applicants, if not more. Whether or not a given applicant possesses potential for further growth is another matter, but such potential can be as much a liability as an asset if promotional opportunities do not match the ambition of the candidate. For the immediate needs, usually quite a few candidates will do, and it may be difficult to place them in rank order.

A second reason for ultra conservatism in the hiring process is because in most instances so little is known about the applicant. The manager has access to academic records, but performance in the classroom usually serves as only a negative criterion and not a positive one. Poor grades may be reason enough not to hire. Good grades, though, still do not tell very much about intelligence, ability to do independent thinking, attitude toward work, dependability and the ability to get along with others. They may not even tell us much about classroom work if there is grade inflation.

Letters of recommendation have, according to recent studies, become less important. Such letters are now legally accessible documents, and—praiseworthy as that development is—it has made the writers of these letters extremely careful not to make negative comments. Some organizations have adopted the practice of confirming for their previous employees only the dates of employment and title held and revealing nothing else. Some prospective employers who have personal contacts at related companies or organizations have taken to telephone follow-ups, on the assumption that comments made on the phone are not documented and therefore may be more frank. The evaluation of letters of recommendation has descended to a search for the positive comments *not* made amidst all the favorable statements, on the rather dubious premise that such an omission is intentional and therefore meaningful.

The third and perhaps most important reason for defensiveness is that protections for the rights of all employees against arbitrary termination, which were properly advanced to eliminate unfair dismissals, may have been extended too far. Many administrators feel that it is difficult if not impossible to get rid of unsatisfactory performers, no matter how well the case may be documented. This in turn quite understandably makes them cautious in hiring. Rather than look to find good candidates they look to spot potentially troublesome ones, using criteria that are at best unsophisticated. The unfortunate result is the frequent elimination from consideration of some very bright candidates who appear somehow different and do not fit the mold. However, without the resurrection of procedures that permit meaningful evaluation at least during the probationary process, little if any improvement can be expected. At present many employers feel pressured to avoid terminating any employee, whatever the reason. This is due to a combination of organizational and societal pressures. As long as it persists or is perceived to exist, supervisors will continue in their own self-interest to minimize problems rather than maximize potential benefits.

The Process of Selection

The process of selecting outside candidates usually consists of a series of steps, each intended to narrow what may be a very large number of applicants to more manageable proportions. The first step consists of a review of the applicant's cover letter. Simple errors, such as misspellings, can serve to eliminate a candidate from consideration. If this appears a trivial ground, it must be remembered that at this stage the task is not to find candidates to consider but rather to find applicants to eliminate.

The second step is consideration of the resume. Here the employer is looking for both positive and negative clues. Positive information that differentiates this candidate from the others will stand out. However, so will information that the reviewer considers negative in this highly subjective process. Most telling are unanswered questions. It may not be clear from the resume just what the individual did between 1978 and 1980 or whether the most recent job assignment involved the supervision of clerks (as required in the present job description). It probably would not be difficult to find answers to these questions, but with 50 applications in hand that do address all questions the reviewer may not be inclined to bother. However, the reviewer may well decide to consider an application from someone who does not directly meet the stated requirements but who stresses alternate equivalent assets.

Different reviewers look for different attributes in evaluating resumes. Some reviewers look for a resume that stresses the unique and positive personality of a candidate; others try to avoid such people. Many look for evidence of determination and dedication demonstrated by volunteer work, even if this experience has nothing to do with the position in question. Still others look for clues to either leadership or social acceptance within a group. Election to office in a professional association obviously provides such an indication, but even the presidency of a social club is helpful. Extra skills, be these languages or familiarity with types of computers or other equipment, may be desirable, especially for stockpilers.

By the time cover letters and resumes have been reviewed, the number of candidates has usually been weeded down to four or five at most. It is at this stage that it becomes useful for the prospective employees to know how many candidates there are and if there are internal candidates. This is particularly important if applicants are supposed to provide their own expenses for travel to the interview or if the employer uses the rather curious but nevertheless not uncommon practice of promising to reimburse only the one successful applicant.

When preparing to select candidates for a final interview, the employer should request letters of recommendation. Asking candidates to submit reference letters along with their initial applications, or requesting them for candidates who may have been rejected before the letters have even arrived, is wasteful.

The Interview

A number of studies have confirmed, in the library field as elsewhere, that the greatest emphasis in the selection process is on the interview itself. Employers or their representatives apparently have confidence in their own judgments, even when they lack confidence in information supplied by others. That self-confidence is not necessarily misplaced. Some of an individual's traits, including the ability to articulate and the ability to interact in a working group, can best be assessed from face-to-face conversation.

It is important for the interviewer to ask questions that will shed light on the applicant's qualifications for the specific job. This requires that the interviewer prepare in advance a statement of what the requirements are and a series of questions designed to elicit relevant information.

At the same time, there are pitfalls in heavy reliance on the interview. Some individuals interview better than others. For some, in fact, the interview finds them at their best, and they will never look that good again. That prospect increases with the proliferation of books and seminars dealing with interview techniques. For some individuals the interview may begin to resemble a role in a play, with little if any resemblance to reality. Others, of course, because of a lack of self-confidence, a lack of experience in interviewing, or perhaps because of a slight speech impediment that would make very little difference for some jobs, interview badly. The wise interviewer allows for all these factors, so as not to be influenced one way or the other by irrelevancies. Unfortunately, many interviewers are just as bad at the process as the candidates they are interviewing.

Management literature has for some time acknowledged the "halo effect" in interpersonal communications, and the halo effect is nowhere more in evidence than during the brief employment interview. Simply put, the halo effect is a predisposition toward an applicant based on some aspect of the individual's appearance, personality or background, the influence of which far exceeds its real importance. Halo effects can work both positively and negatively. People can will themselves into liking someone they are predisposed to favor, and they can find reasons to reject an individual whom they have already rejected emotionally. Rarely is the interviewer aware of the subjective nature of his or her judgment. Having reached an emotional conclusion, it is not difficult to develop a rationale to support it. The greatest risk of being influenced by the halo effect takes place in the job interview situation. If the halo effect has had a negative impact, there will be no opportunity for second thoughts or reevaluations. If the impact has been unreasonably positive, then the manager may be stuck with the results of either his own impetuous judgment or the opinion of the person to whom the hiring decision has been assigned.

The halo effect in employment decisions is bad precisely because it tends to distract us from proper bases for judgment and lure us toward irrelevant ones. Whether an applicant's attire at the interview is "tasteful" is probably completely irrelevant, in part because the individual probably will not dress on the job as for the interview, and because a gently made suggestion will usually be heeded. We therefore run the risk both of employing unqualified candidates because "we like them" or because they remind us of someone we like, and of rejecting other candidates because of some mannerism.

Equal Opportunity Employment

Choosing employees on the basis of the halo effect can have even more serious and perhaps even legal implications. Discrimination against minority groups, the elderly and one or the other sex is sometimes willful and deliberate, but much of it is unconscious. The judgment that someone "would not fit in" or "would not like it here" because of age, race or sex is irrelevant for the employer. It may or may not be an issue for the applicant to be the only male, the only black or the only employee over 35 within the organization, but that is the applicant's decision to make. It is not the employer's. In fact, it is the supervisor's responsibility to ensure that such "different" individuals are afforded a fair opportunity in the workplace. In rare cases the injunction must be forcefully presented to the other employees. A manufacturing corporation that integrated its work force in the early 1960s made the point very effectively. People would not be forced to work in the company of another person in whose presence they felt uncomfortable. They could quit.

Affirmative action programs to combat the effects of past discrimination may accelerate the achievement of equal opportunity, or they may thwart both fairness and the hiring of competent employees. Much depends on the individual supervisor and on the attitudes established within the organization. A great deal depends on how affirmative action is approached. Generally, the use of quotas or even of targets which are difficult to distinguish from quotas can be heavy-handed and simplistic, because these place results ahead of process.

Two arguments frequently raised in support of affirmative action programs are that some of the tests and selection criteria in use are without relevance, and that salary policies discriminate against women, minorities and other groups with lower salary histories. There is merit in both allegations.

Determining Initial Salary

In making salary offers it is a common practice to pay whatever amount it takes to get an individual to accept. A rule of thumb calls for offering between 10% and 15% over what the individual is earning, and personnel officers are inclined to try it. However, if inequities exist, such an action simply perpetuates them. Once an individual is hired, further salary increases are normally calculated as percentages of the base salary. Thus, inequities compound themselves. If one individual is earning $15,000 and another $20,000, a 10% salary increase for both will widen the gap from $5000 to $5500.

There is only one meaningful approach to salary inequity. People should be paid what the job they are expected to perform is worth, regardless of salary history. This requires discipline at both extremes. If the appropriate salary for a job is $20,000, then an individual earning $15,000 should be offered that amount, even though some personnel administrators will figure that the candidate would happily accept $16,500. Conversely, an individual already earning $22,000 should not be considered at all, unless there are clear reasons why the candidate might accept $20,000 and not feel resentful.

Using Tests

The pertinence or irrelevancy of tests also raises significant issues of policy. There is no doubt that some tests have a cultural bias. As an example, the Graduate Record Examination is not only difficult for students whose native language is not English, it is even looked at with suspicion by English-speaking Canadians.

Some tests are clearly relevant to certain jobs. For a secretary, for example, the ability to type to specific standards and the ability to spell are important. One who cannot pass tests of these skills is unsuitable, regardless of why the individual is not able to spell common English words. Similarly, for a job that requires heavy telephone contact, the employer can reasonably ask applicants to demonstrate speech patterns in English comprehensible to others in the organization or to clients.

Proper balance in the hiring process is difficult to maintain precisely because of such interfering factors as the halo effect and a fascination with irrelevant tests and statistical indicators.

Where tests are not relevant they should not be administered at all. Library administrators have long ago, and mercifully, moved away from giving clerical aptitude tests to prospective librarians. It is of course useful for librarians to be able to type, but only in the same sense as it is useful for journalists—as a communications device. The development of computer terminals has slightly altered that skill requirement; the evolution of voice-sensitive input equipment may eliminate it entirely. If a test is required and the existing vehicle is suspected of having a cultural or ethnic bias, or of being outdated, then a better test for all candidates must be developed. It is not satisfactory to administer a test, and then ignore the results because we do not care for them. If test standards are more favorable to some applicants than to others, then we must find other ones by which everyone can be judged equally.

SUMMARY

Managers must develop criteria for evaluation and selection that are fair and free from bias. To the extent that both an individual's potential and performance become factors in the evaluation, making allowances for special circumstances is fair. A former secretary who has been away from the work force for 15 years cannot be expected to be able to take shorthand at 120 words per minute as she or he once did, but it might be reasonable to anticipate an improvement to that level within a period of weeks or months of renewed activity.

Under no circumstances should managers reject their own best judgment and accept a candidate that someone else urges them to hire for reasons of convenience, politics or even affirmative action. It has never been suggested that affirmative action be used to employ unqualified candidates, or even to employ less qualified candidates. It can and should be used to provide opportunity to individuals with potential who have not had the opportunity to demonstrate it. However, the supervisor must always have a reasonable underlying expectation of success. Giving people jobs they cannot handle is unfair to the organization, its employees and the other candidates, but it is particularly unfair to the ones who are selected improperly and who are thus set on the road to failure.

The process of selection also requires rejection. There is usually no painless way to inform applicants that they did not get the job, but failing to tell them at all is far worse. Some individuals are eliminated early in the search process, and there is no fair reason not to tell them at that point. In addition, all candidates have a right to know the time frame for reaching a decision, the mechanism for notifying all candidates and some realistic assessment of their chances if they are brave enough to inquire.

The proper administration of selection and hiring requires basic fairness, a concentration on relevant rather than irrelevant considerations, a willingness to make decisions, and the courage to make the right decisions even in the face of opposition. It is no coincidence that all these characteristics have already been enumerated as qualities needed by all good managers.

8

Career Development, Training and Continuing Education

THE CONCEPT OF CAREER DEVELOPMENT

Career development, in libraries as in other organizational settings, is a fairly recent concept which goes back at most 30 years. Prior to that time little attention was paid to the development of individual employees except within the framework of the organization's needs. That kind of development program still exists; for example, when a library sends an employee to learn more about the use of the MARC systems for serials management, it does so to fulfill organizational needs. The action might also be beneficial to the employee, and it might also enhance career development to the extent that it makes him or her more valuable in the present organization or more attractive to a new one. However, the motivation for the decision was not career development, it was organizational need.

Career development and a concentration on the needs and preferences of individuals is something quite different. It may indeed have benefits for the organization, although this is not as automatic as some behavioral scientists would have us believe. Career development, as opposed to job development, fits the needs and preferences of individuals, and as we have already postulated throughout this book, individuals differ and defy simple categorization.

Pressures for career development programs evolved in large part from the increased emphasis on the quality of working life that prevailed in the 1960s and 1970s. Activists sought jobs that provided more of a sense of personal accomplishment, a greater degree of freedom and greater opportunities for both personal and professional growth. It should be recalled, though, that even the most repetitive and simple job can be made meaningful if the employee understands the need for the task, the importance of quality and quantity standards, and the contribution he or she is making to the overall organizational objectives. For some employees, career development provides no benefits or incentives, and some even consider it a threat to an environment in which they feel quite comfortable.

Nevertheless, career development programs have become an important feature of the workplace, and many employees will insist on them. The rise of equal employment and affirmative action programs has given particular emphasis to such tendencies. Confronted by the strong desire, or even legal necessity, to provide advancement opportunities for members of minority groups, while at the same time attempting to avoid placing people in jobs they cannot perform, managements have turned increasingly to formal career development plans. It can be argued that to a great extent such programs have strong potential benefits for the organization. They avoid the danger of future obsolescence, particularly in the face of new technology. They provide new skills that can be stockpiled for future needs. Finally, career development programs can be shown to be helpful in employee retention. In many cases, employees who are induced by career development programs to stay at a company are also highly motivated toward achievement and recognition.

JUSTIFYING CAREER DEVELOPMENT PROGRAMS

Career development programs are particularly difficult for libraries to implement. So are training and continuing education programs, which will be discussed later in this chapter. All of them involve an investment today for which the payoff, if indeed there is a payoff, comes some time in the future. In dealing with issues of the quality of work life and dignity of the individual, no economic justification need be made, although some have attempted to do so with dubious results.

Career development and other programs which have invested resources in employee training are difficult for any organization lacking commitment of higher management to clearly articulated objectives and goals. Libraries in many large bureaucratic settings are not perceived to have independent objectives except as subsets of the goals and objectives identified for the parent body. In many cases, this becomes translated for the library into pressures which are very short-term. For example, in an academic library the major, or perhaps only, objective established by the faculty or administration may be the purchase of a large number of books and their availability for use.

Libraries have had difficulty, in virtually all settings, in having the librarians' longer-term objectives outrank the short-term demands of their users or the political structures to which they report. Libraries still tend to operate in an atmosphere of crisis, moving from one emergency to the next; such an environment is not very conducive to the evolution of staff career development, which is based either on more general value considerations or projected payoffs in a much longer-term time frame.

What the Individual Wants

At the same time, it must be borne in mind that, in spite of the desirability of promoting career development programs, it would be a mistake to force them on everyone. As we have previously noted, concepts of job expansion and job rotation, or those of participation in the decision process, are often implemented using generalizations about what *all* employees want. The only generalization to which we can adhere is that people need to feel that their work is important, and that what they do and how they feel matters. Even the popular "Theory Z," generally attributed to William Ouchi[1] and based on his research about Japanese management practice, relies fundamentally on the establishment of a climate in which organizational goals and objectives are understood and accepted, and in which the employee recognizes the importance of his or her contribution. While Ouchi and others may stress the importance of allowing for employee participation in the decision process, such an environment must also emphasize overall employee involvement in control over his or her own job and how it is performed, rather than have all related determinations dictated by organizational policies.

In library settings as elsewhere, each individual will react differently to opportunities for career development. Writers such as Van Maanen and Schein[2] have indicated that many people follow broadly defined career stages. These include the exploration stage, in which the individual tests his or her ability to work and accomplish real vocational tasks; the early career establishment stage, which includes job change, transfer, promotion and leveling off; the maintenance stage, which usually includes the greatest period of increasing responsibilities but within an already established career pattern; and ultimately the decline stage, in which the individual accepts and sometimes actively seeks a reduced role, plans for retirement and establishes new priorities based on family, friends and community.

All these career stages are likely to be represented in a library staff, and although there is a relationship between age and experience and the specific stage an employee may be going through, the relationship is not automatic. There are individuals in their 50s and 60s who still seek career development and job expansion, and there are those in their 20s and 30s who have already begun to make the transfer in priorities to other values.

It is important that career development be presented as an opportunity and never as a requirement or threat. It is perfectly acceptable for an individual to perform satisfactorily in a position without seeking either development or advancement, and such people should never be browbeaten or embarrassed into accepting promotions they do not want. It is equally important that they understand the limitations imposed by the choices they have made. The chapter on performance evaluation will deal with this issue in greater detail.

TRAINING AND EDUCATION REQUIREMENTS

Although "education" and "training" are sometimes used interchangeably or even as the compound word "educationand-training" in library parlance, they have distinct meanings. In general, education is a broadly based intellectual preparation in conceptual understanding, issues and the ability to analyze and judge. Training, as differentiated from education, is far more narrow. It involves the learning of knowledge or skills for a specific purpose. That purpose is directly related to work to be performed. Training, as opposed both to career development and education, is job-specific and can be shown to have a much more immediate impact on the accomplishment of organizational objectives on a day-to-day basis.

Education

Not all jobs in libraries require the same educational base. Clerical tasks involving little intellectual judgment, analysis or planning can frequently be performed by people with just a high school education, even though the specific job skills may be highly developed. This will be true as long as the tasks are routine or based on specific ground rules. In general, it is assumed that professional work in libraries requires at least a masters degree in library or information science. Certain positions require additional masters degrees or even doctorates.

Accreditation processes exist to measure institutional performance, and other tools are also available to the employer seeking to evaluate the quality of the applicant's library education background. This book will have little to say about the educational process, because I share the view that basically education must be acquired in an academic setting, and cannot be acquired through experience in the workplace.

Equivalency tables for education and experience have been established in the development of job descriptions. (These issues will be discussed in a later chapter.) In general, though, job experience provides training at best and rarely education. It is not even certain that longevity implies extensive training. In determining training and experience standards it is necessary to differentiate between what may be seven years of experience on the one hand and, on the other hand, working for seven years but coming out with only one year of experience repeated seven times. Not only library supervisors, but even the far more experienced personnel administrators have difficulty in making that distinction. Unfortunately, pressures to achieve a desired level of promotion can blur the distinction between education and even training as contrasted to just being there for a certain period of time. The author uses the word "unfortunate" because the greatest victim in this process is the improperly promoted employee. This book will leave the process of education to writings on this topic, although the determination of what education should contain is an issue that requires ongoing discussion between educators and practitioners in the library field. What education should *not* be is training, although in reality educators do more training than they would care to admit. They probably will never do enough, however, to satisfy harried library managers.

Training

Just as daily crisis management makes the creation of career development plans difficult, it also inhibits programs for employee training. The reasons for training programs are largely self-evident. Fundamentally, training is done: 1) to reduce learning time for tasks to be performed on the job; 2) to improve performance on a job in which the employee is already engaged; 3) to improve the attitude of individuals toward their work, largely by giving them a better understanding of what they are doing and why they are doing it; and 4) to solve operational problems in the performance of certain tasks.

In libraries, training, as opposed to education, is usually undertaken on the job. The trainer is usually the immediate supervisor, although in some libraries the personnel department conducts training sessions. It is also not unusual to bring in contractors or vendors to conduct training, particularly when the skills to be imparted are complex or newly developed. The trained employee then can become the internal trainer of others. Such an approach is frequently used when training involves computer-based operations such as online searching, for which no incumbent staff member may be qualified.

Few organizations would argue against the need for training, and few managers would suggest that it could be dispensed with. At the same time, there is a general reluctance to provide training, and that reluctance is clearly evidenced in a number of studies (including one in which I have recently participated[3]). Training takes time and therefore also takes money. Either supervisors must conduct the training themselves, staff specialists must be developed for this purpose or outsiders must be brought in. In any case, there is both a cost incurred and a diversion from the day-to-day production activities that are, in the view of many of the library's users and higher level managers, the library's *raison-d'etre*.

Some other types of organizations accept the cost of training as a normal everyday expense. Chemical and accounting firms hire newly minted graduates in their fields who have already been educated in the basics, and then spend as much as a year or more training them in the specific job skills the organization requires. During much of that period the new hires are not productive, and during part of it they may be negatively productive because they not only produce little of use but also take up the time of their trainer.

Should Training Be Part of Education?

Libraries, have had considerable historic difficulty in accepting and budgeting for the training role and cost. They assume in many cases that a newly hired cataloger or reference librarian can be turned loose on the backlog of monographs or online searches by noon of the first day on the job. The only way to achieve this "luxury" is to have even junior candidates pre-trained by the institutions which were supposed to have educated them. The pressures on such educational institutions then encompass (in addition to education) the imposition of both training and practice work experience as part of the educational curriculum. That approach is found to some extent in such fields as elementary education and medicine. However, in those cases it is intended as an application of educational preparation in an operational setting, and it usually follows the completion of at least a major portion of the educational programs.

If libraries insist that professionals come to them already trained as well as educated, several equally unattractive by-products are possible. The insistence on training, in the finite time environment of the professional schools, inevitably takes place at the expense of education. Another approach involves the practice of hiring individuals with experience for junior-level posts that do not require it. This practice persists because individuals with experience are usually already pre-trained and can tackle their job assignments or the backlogs more rapidly.

It is interesting to note a split between the broad educational values that major library administrators stress and the training experiences for which the first-level supervisors often search when they hire. The split results from the fact that these immediate supervisors recognize, probably correctly, what their own job pressures and priorities are, despite any conflicting rhetoric from their bosses.

The problem is further complicated by the fact that many graduates move directly into posts in school, special, public and even academic libraries in which they are the only professionals. There is nobody to train them. Furthermore, there is probably nobody to determine whether their educational or intellectual preparation is adequate, only whether the work gets done.

The problems are complex and defy simple solutions. At the same time, the search for acceptable professional standards is essential, despite the continuing but unacceptable pressures to do more with less against which Hedberg has warned so effectively.[4] Librarians must never allow their needs and objectives to be subverted by daily pressures applied by others who neither understand nor care and who cannot be realistically expected to do either.[5]

CONTINUING EDUCATION

However, issues of education and training, and opportunities for career development do not end our management problems. Librarianship, like many other fields heavily affected by technological innovation, cannot survive by clinging to the status quo. Professional librarians, no matter how well educated and trained, will quickly become obsolete if they do not continue to learn. We are not alone in facing this dilemma. The medical profession understands it well enough. Doctors prepared 20 years ago without knowledge of new drugs, surgical procedures and methods of treatment cannot possibly provide first-rate service today. Neither can similarly isolated librarians and other information professionals.

While training may have an end point, education in a professional environment rarely does, and this is particularly true in a profession as subject to modification by technology and societal value shifts as librarianship. One of the characteristics of a profession is a process of continued learning. It is therefore disturbing to see that some people look at the library degree or other means of achieving initial professional status as something of a union card, with more learning encouraged but nothing demanded.

Continuing education can be provided through a variety of sources. Educational institutions—in many cases the same ones that provide initial education—offer advanced degree programs, courses, workshops and seminars. The second most popular source is professional societies, which offer workshops and seminars usually lasting one or two days, frequently in conjunction with annual conferences and meetings. It is common for such professional societies to offer certificates of continuing education units for completion of such programs, although the success of the learning process is rarely tested. Also available are continuing education experiences offered by federal, state and local governments, and by equipment vendors and systems organizations. These last types may be valuable, but they are usually oriented to the specific product or service supplied by the teaching organization, and must therefore be evaluated for relevance to the specific setting.

Financing Training and Continuing Education

In general, the success of continuing education programs depends on both money and motivation. The program can be funded directly by the employer, which is the most common approach used in industry. It can be supported by a government agency, although at the time this book is being written little likelihood seems to exist of a return to the level of government support available in the 1960s. Continuing education can be underwritten by the university or professional society providing it. Again, this is unlikely, because of the requirements for cost recovery that are besetting these groups. Finally, the cost can be borne by the individual; this is the model used most commonly for the continuing education of schoolteachers during the summer months. Discussion of this alternative leads to the consideration of personal motivation.

The costs of continuing education are not trivial. Enrollment in a university course might cost anywhere from $180 to $600. One-day continuing education seminars offered by professional societies in the library field are usually priced at about $75 to $100 for a six-hour session. In the management field they are several times greater. To the financial cost must be added the time involved, borne either by the employer if the educational experience takes place during the working day, or by the individual if it occurs in the evening or on the weekend.

Motivating for Continuing Education

The motivation for individuals to invest their own time and money in the continuing education process is largely based on the old adage of the carrot (inducement) or the stick (threat). Inducement for continuing education comes in the form of promised salary increases, promotions or at least promotional opportunities on the completion of a course, series of courses or degree program. This is the model largely used in school systems, where union contracts frequently provide specific salary increases tied to the completion of educational units. Clearly, inducements are preferable to threats, but even threats have their place. Retaining one's present job may require updating of knowledge and skills through continuing education programs.

Neither mechanism now works well in the library field.[6] The threat of termination for failure to complete continuing education units is not attractive in any case. The Medical Library Association has initiated evaluations tied to the certification process, but in settings involving either civil service, tenure or union contracts such a step would be completely unacceptable. The promise of reward in return for continuing education does not work well in the library field, either. There is little evidence of promotion, salary increase, or even of favorable consideration for either of these in return for the investment in continuing education. Relying on the motivation of self-gratification may seem to be the most attractive of all the alternatives, but evidence shows that it touches only a small number of individuals.

The most direct means for ensuring continuing education is to make it a normal part of the job and to include its cost in both dollars and time in the organizational budget. Very little of this occurs at present, in any kind of library setting. There is some indication of a tendency to release time, under which the employer absorbs the time away from the job but not the dollars. However, in a professional setting even such a "gift" may be a poisoned apple, if the individual is expected to make up for lost time by working evenings and weekends.

Making continuing education, together with training and career development, a part of the planned and budgeted expenditure of the library will not be easy, given budgetary pressures and the lack of awareness by others that librarianship even involves such processes. But it is the only reasonable approach. It gives the organization some control over the direction of training and continuing education. It must be part of the planning strategy of administrators, and it must be incorporated in the statements of the library's goals and objectives.

At times of rising expectations and increasing complexity, individuals like organizations must improve to just keep pace. If they do not improve, they automatically get weaker.

NOTES

1. Ouchi, William, *Theory Z: How American Business Can Meet the Japanese Challenge* (Reading, MA: Addison-Wesley, 1981).

2. Van Maanen, John, and Schein, Edgar H., "Career Development." In *Improving Life at Work,* edited by J. Richard Hackman and J. Lloyd Suttle (Santa Monica, CA: Goodyear Publishing Co., 1977).

3. White, Herbert S., and Paris, Marion, "Employer Preferences and the Library Education Curriculum," *Library Quarterly* (January 1985).

4. Hedberg, Bo, et al., "Camping on Seesaws. Prescriptions for a Self-Designing Organization," *Administrative Science Quarterly* 21(1) (1976):41-65.

5. White, Herbert S., "Subverted by Pragmatism," *Library Journal* 109 (May 1, 1984):861-862.

6. White, Herbert S., and Paris, Marion, "Employer Preferences and the Library Education Curriculum," *Library Quarterly* (January 1985).

9

Job Design and Employee Evaluation

HISTORIC APPROACHES TO JOB DESIGN

The historic approach to job design, in libraries and elsewhere, was based on the models developed by Frederick Taylor and other champions of scientific management. The steps used in this conventional approach, still found in some libraries, included the following:

1) Break the job into the smallest possible component to reduce skill requirements.

2) Make it as repetitive as possible to reduce the need for decisions and interpretation.

3) Minimize handling and transportation. Let workers stay at the workplace, and bring the work to them. The assembly line is the most obvious example of this idea, but catalogers who are expected to stay at their desks while the supervisor brings work to them function in a similar environment.

4) Provide suitable working conditions for the job, not necessarily for the employee. Typing pools, with all personnel concentrated in one location for ease of supervision and work assignments, are an example.

5) Obtain greater specialization and do not waste skills once learned.

6) Stabilize production into a consistent flow. For library cataloging departments dependent on the receipt of variable mail shipments, this means the establishment of planned backlogs, so that nobody will ever run out of work. Sometimes, the backlogs get out of hand. Stabilized production is more difficult to establish in reference departments, which depend for their work on walk-in clients or ringing telephones, and here the approach has been to establish "busy work" for each employee, to be performed when other activity was low.

The emphasis in all these steps was to waste nothing in the way of resources, be these skills, materials, money or time. As mentioned, parts of this approach remain in effect in a large number of libraries. Nevertheless, by the 1960s changes began to be evident and both behavioral scientists and managers started to question the appropriateness of such techniques for a work force with greater education and higher expectations for job satisfaction and job involvement than had once been common. One of the earliest pioneers in this endeavor was Frederick Herzberg, who provided a theoretical formulation for job enrichment. Favorable results with job enrichment experiments were claimed in terms of quality and quantity of production, attendance, costs and morale. New job designs including job enlargement, job rotation and the establishment of work teams soon followed. These changes have been welcomed by many librarians, who have come to expect a greater sense of involvement and participation. Others, who felt secure in the knowledge of what was expected from each task, felt threatened.

There is no clear evidence to support the financial benefits that were claimed. In general, both productivity and attendance have continued to decline, but many factors contribute to this phenomenon. Library managers, like managers in other organizations, must be prepared to deal with employees' continuing desire for more interesting and meaningful work, while assuring themselves that this is still work that indeed needs to be performed. At the same time, these managers must also continue to deal with subordinates who do not welcome these changes, and who feel threatened by them.

JOB DESIGN TODAY

Despite the doubters and recalcitrants, job design is rapidly coming to encompass the following characteristics:

1) Greater employee control over one's own work and how it is performed, with evaluation based on results and not on methods.

2) Opportunities for social interaction. Early 20th-century efficiency experts sought to isolate employees in the belief that contact encouraged irrelevant social conversation on job time. Such a perception may indeed have been correct, but the work force developed in the affluent and individualistic 1960s would not tolerate such restrictions. The simplistic assumption of an eight-hour work day minus two fifteen minute coffee breaks quickly changed to the realization that six and sometimes only five productive hours in a work day was a more realistic expectation around which to build schedules.

More recently one of the major employee complaints about the installation of computer terminals at work stations is that this development has hampered socialization and given management the capability for monitoring productive time. It is argued that these new technological changes have dehumanized the workplace, but a more cynical response would be that they have reestablished criteria for assuring that individuals work when they are supposed to work.

3) The opportunity to produce whole units of work and thus to promote a sense of accomplishment. It is this sense of contribution and accomplishment (not necessarily based on an ability to control) which is central to the development of work teams, and to the evolution of Japanese management philosophy.

4) Utilization of a variety of skills, to provide both learning experience and growth, and to avoid boredom.

5) The provision of feedback to the employee, so that his or her work can be considered within the overall perspective of

organizational goals and objectives. The employee must have some understanding of what difference his or her being there and trying made.

What Employees Want

This trend of changes in job design fits well with the expectations of employees with regard to their own jobs. Five such expectations can be stated as generalizations, and they are neither confrontational nor unreasonable. There are obviously some employees who want more. These five, though, represent a common denominator, and library managers would be well-advised to bear them in mind.

1) *Let us make sure we (supervisor and employee) both understand what it is you expect of me.* This is not a confrontational employee statement. It does not demand, as some individuals might indeed demand, a voice in the development of job descriptions and standards of job performance. It asks only for an understanding of the ground rules, of the expectations against which performance will be judged. In its simplest terms it asks, "What is my job?" It is sad that such a reasonable request must be made at all. However, many workers in libraries and other organizations do not know what their jobs are. Nobody has told them, and in turn this may be because the supervisor is not sure, either. Alternatively, it may be because the supervisor wants to reserve the right to change the ground rules with each new assignment. It is an intolerable circumstance in either case.

2) *Leave me alone.* Many psychological studies have established the strongly felt need for a personal territory, for a place of one's own. In the workplace this can mean having one's own desk or at least one's own drawers in a shared desk. The fact that one of the most widely recognized rewards in the workplace is a private office is a recognition of this need. This feeling also applies to the job itself. An employee has the right to say, "Having given me a job to do, leave me alone and let me do it." Many well-meaning supervisors smother their subordinates to protect them from making mistakes. (An extreme example, from a case study in the

library literature, is a supervisor who hovers over a cataloger correcting mistakes as they are made.)

Subordinates deserve the right to organize and perform their own work within the limits of prescribed guidelines. These guidelines should focus not on method but on results to be accomplished. This right to individual freedom includes the right to be allowed to make some mistakes. Employees who perceive that no mistake will ever be tolerated will cease to think and simply will follow orders, no matter how pointless or mistaken these may seem.

3) *Help me if I ask for help.* This is not a contradiction of the above point. Subordinates should of course be encouraged to ask questions if they are not sure of what they should be doing. Creating an atmosphere in which they feel it is safer to guess can cause monumental foul-ups and substantial delays. If subordinates feel that questions are not encouraged, they will stop asking them. They will either sit and do nothing because they do not know what to do, or they will make assumptions and guesses which might be totally wrong. However, it is sometimes appropriate in the process of providing an answer to point out how a future question (never the present one) might be avoided.

4) *Tell me how I did.* Individuals want to know how they did, or at least what you think of their performance. They would obviously prefer praise to criticism. However, they will accept criticism if it appears fair, and if it is couched in constructive terms. At a minimum, if a supervisor is dissatisfied with a subordinate's performance, that individual should be told, particularly if the supervisor's opinion will be the basis for a decision concerning promotion, salary adjustment or retention.

5) *Reward me in accordance with how I did.* This is a reasonable expectation. However, because some supervisors lack either the ability or the courage to reward or punish based on performance, subordinates frequently complain that they are not told how they did. Tying salary and other reward systems to performance is important for two reasons. First of all, money is an impor-

tant motivator for most people. The second reason is that individuals are suspicious of easy praise, particularly if it is distributed lavishly to everyone. Talk is cheap and is perceived to be. The next chapter will discuss in more detail the use of salary policy as an inducement or as a threat. For the moment it will suffice to note that subordinates look at rewards tied to performance evaluation (tell me how I did) as a sign of sincerity, as an indication that the supervisor really meant what he or she said. An egalitarian system of rewards carries the seeds of its own dilution of quality. The worst employees, happy at being treated "equally," will gladly stay. The best employees, and particularly those who have been told they are the best, will seek rewards for their excellence elsewhere.

Given these straightforward expectations of subordinates for the design and evaluation of their jobs, one may well wonder why the tasks are performed so badly. Job design and performance evaluation, which could have such a positive influence, instead often cause resentment and agitation.

Ideally, the design of a job should meet the needs of both the organization and the individual. In a library this matching of aims is particularly difficult, because neither the supervisor nor the employee usually sees specific jobs in terms of the accomplishment of stated objectives.

Guidelines for Writing Job Descriptions

Letting the process of developing job descriptions begin by allowing individuals to describe what they think they do, and perhaps what they think they ought to do, is not unreasonable, but the process cannot be allowed to end there. In developing their own job descriptions subordinates may or may not relate to what is supposed to happen, or to what can reasonably be expected. Also, they may de-emphasize tasks they do not enjoy.

Job descriptions must relate to a task or series of tasks which need to be performed in carrying out the objectives and programs of the library. Individual tasks are adapted to organization needs, *not* organizational priorities to individual preferences. If individuals know what the organizational needs are and what the relationship is between them and their jobs, that point is usually accepted without question.

It is indeed a foolish supervisor who does not at least attempt some sort of match or accommodation between employee preferences and necessary work, but only to a reasonable extent. In smaller libraries there is far less leeway than in larger ones. If there is only one reference librarian, then that individual must shoulder all of the required tasks, including the ones that are enjoyed as well as those that are not. The supervisor must then be alert to the possibility that undesired tasks may be put off in favor of those considered more enjoyable.

Ultimately, the job description developed must present a clear and unambiguous delineation of what is to be done. It must include enough specific yardsticks so that the subordinate can evaluate whether he or she is performing the job satisfactorily, even before being told by the supervisor. Job description statements such as "and other duties as may be assigned" are undoubtedly necessary to permit unforeseen modification, but when these "other duties" begin to take up a major part of the effort, the job description has become meaningless and must be restructured.

Fitting people to jobs rather than jobs to people obviously carries the risk of some unpleasant discoveries. You may find either that the individual is in a job he or she cannot perform, or perhaps that the library has no job suited to what this individual can do, even taking into account the potential of training and continuing education. Traumatic as such a disclosure may be, its recognition and necessary subsequent action is far preferable to whatever alternative may be perceived. An important guideline for the supervisor is to remember never to lie to himself or herself about the reality of performance evaluation, and never to lie to the employee. The unfortunate victim of a situation in which an individual cannot hope to be successful in his or her job is not the library as much as the employee, whose time and life are now being wasted.

In such a situation it is incumbent on the supervisor to do something: training where this is appropriate and deemed to have a reasonable expectation of success, transfer where this is appropriate and, if necessary, termination.

PERFORMANCE EVALUATION

As already noted, performance evaluation is an essential part of effective personnel administration. It meets the needs of the organization and those of the subordinate, who wants to know how he or she is performing and what will happen as a result of the evaluation. Despite these matching needs, performance evaluation is more often than not done sketchily, hypocritically and meaninglessly, and employees view it is a thinly disguised rationalization for salary and promotional decisions already reached.

Purposes of Performance Evaluation

Performance evaluation, when carried out correctly, meets several important needs. First, it serves to create and maintain satisfactory levels of performance, where the criteria for "satisfactory" are defined in a job description clearly understood by both the supervisor and subordinate.

Performance evaluation also indicates areas for needed or potential growth and development. It does this by pointing not only to needed improvements within the confines of the present job but also to logical extensions of growth and advancement in job scope, job title or both. As already noted, job enrichment and job growth are important criteria for many employees, and a frank discussion of them and the rewards to be expected is a natural part of performance evaluation. Promises of promotion or salary increase should never be made specific if they depend on the existence of a vacancy and the results of a formal search process which includes external candidates. Also, if further personal growth creates capabilities for which the library has no expected use, then it is only fair to tell the employee that.

A third purpose of performance evaluation is to force the supervisor to take at least some interest in the work of the subordinate. The very need to make this point is unfortunate, because supervisor interest tied only to the annual process of performance evaluation is inadequate. However, many supervisors, and particularly those who perform as working supervisors alongside their subordinates, find little or no time for carrying out what is clearly their most important duty. Invariably, this is because of preference rather than need; supervision makes these supervisors uncomfortable. The performance evaluation process at least forces them to do their assigned work some of the time.

Fourth, performance evaluation is a guide to job change. Job descriptions, even those that are correct at the time they are written, must be modified as task assignments change, either because of shifting organizational objectives or priorities, or because of the impact of new technology. Performance evaluation provides an ideal opportunity to review and perhaps revise the job description, particularly when there is no mechanism for doing this automatically.

A final, and vital, purpose of performance evaluation is to provide a guide to fair wage and salary administration. The fifth expectation of subordinates listed above, "Reward me in accordance with how I did," comes into play here. Correctly administered performance evaluation exposes insincere praise or flattery for the fraud it is.

Guidelines for Administering Performance Evaluation

As noted in the introduction to this book, a great deal of the personnel management literature is devoted to techniques and tactics for performance evaluation. Therefore, only points of particular importance to librarians will be dealt with here.

An important detail to remember at all times is that skills the candidate may possess, but which are irrelevant to the job assigned, have no place in the evaluation process.

Some library managers do not realize that performance evaluation is important. It takes time to do it effectively, and the effort is well spent. Where supervisors are reluctant to take the process seriously, it is because they either do not perceive its importance, have not been so charged by their own management or are reluctant to face the unpleasant tasks that performance evaluation sometimes requires. While it is gratifying to be able to tell employees they are doing well, it is less pleasant—but certainly no less important—to tell them when they are doing badly.

Performance evaluation should be an important part of the library's value system, and should be perceived as such by everyone involved. While the process and its results are inevitably controlled by management, it is not intended and does not work well as a monologue. The employee has the right to offer suggestions, to express disagreements and to have these opinions formally documented as a part of the record.

While performance evaluation includes elements of review, the primary purpose of the process is not to discuss the past but to discuss the future. In a proper managerial atmosphere, correction as well as praise will have taken place on a continuing basis throughout the year. It makes little sense to "save up" criticisms concerning poor performance, unsatisfactory attitudes or excessive absenteeism. These concerns should be communicated as they arise, always in a setting which insures privacy and dignity and, if necessary, with appropriate written documentation. The formal performance evaluation should concentrate on the future. It should include changed performance expectations for the present job, perhaps as affected by technology, or changing objectives or programs. It may even include a complete restructuring of the present job and must therefore address new requirements and rewards. The issues of additional training and education must also be discussed.

The performance evaluation setting also provides an ideal opportunity to determine the employee's interest in advancement. If the employee wants to be promoted then the evaluation should include discussion of the criteria and opportunities for promotion. Promotion must be understood to be a process based both on the interests and abilities of the employee and the needs of the organization. It is not an automatic process.

PROMOTION

One of the happiest tasks of any manager is relaying the good news of promotion. An offer of promotion represents confidence and recognition by management, and opportunity and financial reward for the employee. It usually entails an increase in salary, frequently a larger office and other perquisites, and invariably higher recognition by one's peers. Even this process, though, is fraught with dangers.

The offer of a promotion is usually based on superior performance. However, excellence in the present job should not be the sole basis for promotion, although much of the time it is. Promotion should be based primarily on the expectation that the individual has the skills, preparation and personality necessary for success in the new job.

The thoroughness that can make for a very good cataloger can make for a bad supervisor of cataloging, because the supervisor must be able to make decisions based on incomplete evidence. Subordinates who aim for perfection may unrealistically expect that standard of new subordinates after their own promotion, when aiming at perfection may be unnecessary, overly expensive or beyond the capabilities of the new subordinate. It is one of the dangers of working for an individual who once had your job that this individual may expect unrealistic levels of performance not required by the objectives of the organization, and perhaps not achievable by junior employees.

We know from the examination of the characteristics of leaders (and we know that supervisors are expected to be leaders) what to look for in promotion to supervisory rank. Those characteristics are not always directly found in the best cataloger, the best reference librarian or the best circulation clerk.

Promoting individuals solely because of a desire to reward outstanding performance in the present job occurs all too frequently. This practice results in many of the problems that books such as *The Peter Principle* describe. Promotions of this sort may have two disastrous results. They may create unsatisfactory supervisors, and they deprive the organization of its best workers.

Promotions are now used to reward historic performance rather than express a confidence in future performance because most wage and salary systems, and particularly those in libraries, have not developed satisfactory ways to reward outstanding performance without promotion to a management position.

There are at least two more appropriate options. One is to tie the salary to the work quality and quantity being performed. There is no reason why subordinates cannot be paid more highly than their supervisors, but only in the academic faculty system where administrative titles are considered temporary are subordinates ever paid more. It is also possible to develop non-supervisory career tracks, which can represent a variety of values not necessarily including supervisory responsibility. The academic library model of following faculty patterns in appointing assistant, associate and full librarians does not require a formal change in job responsibilities to justify a promotion. Reference librarians who are full librarians can and do report to Heads of Reference who are associate librarians, and there is no reason why this should not be so. They have different responsibilities.

Most individuals nevertheless recognize that the most direct path to status and salary advancement is through the acceptance of management responsibilities. In general, this is not unreasonable, because the impact of a strong manager extends far beyond his or her own daily work. For these reasons, few individuals will turn down a promotion. And yet they should hesitate to accept, because promotion carries with it a risk of failure. Managers are right to tell candidates for promotion why they feel the promotion is a good idea, but it is wrong to pressure the candidates into accepting. In most organizational settings, promotion is a one-way street, and if the new assignment does not work out it is rarely reversible. The expectations and risks in a promotional assignment should be carefully spelled out, but they rarely are. Instead the concentration is on the prestige and on the higher salary. Perhaps, if promotional assignments were based more on expectations and less on historic performance, and if all of the ramifications were clearly spelled out, we would have fewer poor supervisors in our field.

Finally, when a promotion is appropriate, it cannot be unreasonably delayed or denied because the present supervisor deems the candidate too valuable to spare. The irony of such a situation is easily apparent and will also be clear to the luckless candidate, who will leave if possible and resent the entrapment if leaving is not feasible.

TRANSFERS

Transfers can sometimes be useful and can salvage a nonproductive employee. Transfers can be undertaken at the initiation of the employee or of the organization. They can be based on shifts in work load and organizational priorities, and such shifts can be either temporary or permanent. The difference should be clearly understood by all parties. Transfers can also be undertaken if it is discovered that an employee was improperly assigned in the first place, and is occupying a post he or she cannot perform and for which training is not practical. Finally, transfers can be used to overcome personality problems and clashes, which can sometimes destroy a working relationship without anyone being to blame.

Transfers should only be undertaken when, as with promotions, there is a reasonable expectation of success. Problem employees should not be transferred simply to delay the need to deal with the problem. Such a transfer solves nothing, and it is unfair both to the unsuspecting new supervisor and to the employee who is being shunted around the organization. It is far better to deal with the problem of an unsatisfactory employee in his present department, unless one of the criteria spelled out above applies.

DISCIPLINARY ACTION

The premise of all enlightened management systems is the avoidance wherever possible of the need to use management power overtly. First, it is largely unnecessary and redundant, since the subordinate already knows who is in charge. It is indeed a weak supervisor who must constantly remind him. Second, there are many constraints on the authority of the supervisor. Some of these emerged as legitimate limitation on the exercise of arbitrary power. Others emerged from legislation, from court cases, from a desire to avoid adverse publicity and from the sociological approach to management which had such a great influence in the 1960s and 1970s. Constraints on the actions of a supervisor include organizational rules, laws, precedent and sometimes the cowardice of the manager's own superior who may seek to avoid trouble at all cost.

Disciplinary action is therefore avoided when at all possible. Tactics for this include the following:

1) Hire the right people in the first place and take care in the hiring process to avoid problems. That statement is positive on its face value, but care must be taken not to interpret it to mean the avoidance of hiring anyone who differs from the norm. Some who differ from the norm are better, or at least potentially better.

2) Train new hires properly. Make sure they understand their jobs, their responsibilities and performance expectations. Give them the tools they need, and access to needed information if they have questions.

3) Make sure employees understand organizational rules and the consequences for breaking those rules. The United States Army, which still reads the Articles of War to all of its new recruits, is probably an effective manager in at least this instance.

4) Review performance at regular intervals, but deal with problems immediately as they occur.

5) Evaluate and counsel on a continuing basis.

Despite all of these safeguards, problems will occur. One set of problems involves employees who cannot do the work their job requires because:

1) They were improperly hired.

2) They were improperly trained, and there is now no opportunity to retrain.

3) The situation has changed for the employee. Perhaps the employee is no longer as interested or perhaps outside distractions are preventing the employee from concentrating or functioning as expected.

4) The job has changed, and no longer fits the employee and his or her abilities. While retraining is obviously the fairest and most direct action, it will not work all the time. Managers must constantly be reminded that in real work settings nothing works all of the time.

It is clear that such problems must be handled with sensitivity and compassion. Retraining may present an option, or perhaps an appropriate transfer is available.

However, there are two things you cannot do. First, you cannot leave an employee in a job that he or she cannot perform. Second, you cannot, or should not create a job you do not need because it happens to fit an employee you have.

Another set of problems involves employees who will not work or who will not adhere to organizational discipline. Some individuals have made a commitment to avoid productive work and to confront or ignore all rules, although most organizational rules are increasingly permissive and open to interpretation. If you have such subordinates (and most supervisors will at some time) do not consider it your fault. Not everyone is salvageable. These individuals must be weeded from the work group, or at least isolated, or they will poison the working atmosphere. Other subordinates know full well who the individuals are who refuse to contribute, who refuse to come to work on time and who refuse to follow the simplest instructions. They resent (even if secretly admire) what these individuals are getting away with, and they expect management to do something about it.

Again, there are a number of tactics to avoid such a situation, some obviously more effective than others:

1) Don't hire such individuals. Many such candidates provide clues during the interview of their future behavior. There may be an absence of favorable recommendations or an unexplained tendency to change jobs or locations.

2) Weed them out at the end or even before the end of the probationary period. Individuals who will not perform satisfactorily under the threat of probation certainly will not do so after that threat is removed. Almost all organizations have probationary assignments for new employees. Don't be reluctant to avail yourself of that opportunity. If terminating a probationary employee is difficult, it is still considerably easier than terminating a permanent employee.

3) Don't transfer them to another unsuspecting supervisor, pretending that they are really fine. Solve your own problems, and expect others to solve theirs.

4) Don't suspend them. This action, so popular in union grievance situations, accomplishes nothing. The work which has not been done in the employee's presence certainly will not get done in his or her absence, and in all probability you won't be able to use the saved salary funds for any other purpose. The employee returns from suspension in the self-righteous belief that everything is now squared, and that the record has been cleared.

DEALING WITH INADEQUATE PERFORMANCE

When an employee's work is thoroughly inadequate, the performance evaluation process is painful for both the manager and the employee. However, the situation must be faced squarely. It is possible that transfer is the answer. Retraining might work, too. When neither of these solutions is feasible, firing may be necessary.

If the employee cannot be fired—perhaps because of the policy of the organization—the process of performance evaluation can be used to encourage the individual to resign. First, the manager must document the employee's performance shortcomings. The manager must confront the employee with documentation, create a permanent record, inform higher levels of management and determine what it will take to implement disciplinary action. The employee should know what is going on and should be invited to file a grievance, because this will provide the manager with an opportunity to inform others.

Unsatisfactory employees should never be given any raise at all if it can be avoided; if some raise is required, it should be as small as possible.

When all else fails, the manager must plan on how to terminate the employee. Higher-level management and the personnel department must be consulted, but their concerns that firing will be difficult should not govern the situation. Avoiding the problem may be a solution for them, but it is *not* a solution for the unsatisfactory employee's immediate supervisor.

While on occasion such drastic measures will be necessary if the employee is judged to be performing inadequately, given an overall environment in which functions are performed effectively, the process of job descriptions, performance evaluations, promotions and transfers more frequently ties in with the organization's philosophy and program for wage and salary administration. This issue is discussed in the next chapter.

10

Wage and Salary Administration

The implementation of wage and salary policy tends to cause a great deal of difficulty in all organizations, and certainly in libraries. While appropriate salary policies do not necessarily build morale, the absence or perceived absence of fairness can lead to serious and sometimes irreversible morale problems. Employees prefer to *assume* a fair pay system and to concentrate on other job satisfaction issues.

In general, librarians recognize that their profession is not a highly paid one, and they chose their career in spite of its financial shortcomings. As intelligent and rational human beings, they understand that if funds are simply not available, they cannot be distributed. What causes bitter indignation is the belief that their salaries would be higher if management had tried harder or, even worse, if management had at least cared. They want to be paid fairly, at least as they perceive fairness, in comparison to others in like organizations, and particularly to others performing the same tasks.

The insistence "pay me in accordance with how I performed," mentioned earlier, requires a perception of fairness, and a consistency between what the employee is told about his or her work and what is done about it. If individuals have specifically been told they are better performers, they expect to be paid more than others and they expect larger salary increases.

EGALITARIANISM IN SALARY ADMINISTRATION

There has been so much dissatisfaction with the process of salary determination that often individuals settle for an egalitarian system. Such a process, most often found in unionized organizations, involves allotting salary increases and promotions according to a rigid system of rules announced in advance. When promotions are based strictly on seniority, or when terminations or layoffs are based strictly on a lack of seniority, everyone knows exactly where he or she stands. When salary increases are publicly announced or negotiated by union contract, everyone knows exactly what to expect. This egalitarian approach spares the manager the necessity of making hard, subjective decisions. It has so many advantages for the employee and the employer that many kinds of organizations not forced to use it select it voluntarily.

The most obvious examples of this egalitarianism can be found in federal, state and municipal civil service. However, universities also tend toward this approach, and so increasingly do for-profit organizations. During the personnel retrenchment in the automobile industry in the early 1980s, one corporation abandoned its plans to assign layoffs on the basis of quality of performance for professional workers and applied the seniority system specified in the union contract, although there was no such requirement in dealing with professional employees. Layoffs based on lack of seniority are certainly not any more fair than a merit system especially because highly motivated and productive employees may suffer. However, the seniority system is perceived as more fair when the individuals affected do not understand and do not trust the procedures used in a qualitative evaluation system.

Egalitarian systems are fundamentally fair only to egalitarian workers. They are ultimately unsatisfactory to those who are above-average performers, and to the much larger group who think they are. Neither of these groups are satisfied with being treated like everyone else, although they may accept such a system for lack of confidence in a better one. Ultimately, those who perceive themselves as better than average will seek opportunities elsewhere if they can. Some of these people may be the organization's most valued performers.

By contrast, poorer performers will gladly accept the benefit of equal salary adjustments. Egalitarianism, like paternalism (which rewards loyalty rather than performance), weeds out the best. The better people tend to leave, the worse performers tend to stay, and the organization staffing gets progressively worse. This is an unacceptable state for conscientious managers. It can be avoided only by paying people in line with what they contribute.

MERIT PAY SYSTEMS

Ideally, one should be able to avoid the pitfalls of egalitarian pay structures by paying each individual what he or she deserves. Implementing such a merit pay system, however, requires great care.

Problems in Implementing a Merit Pay System

There are two direct and immediate problems in implementing merit pay. First, individuals are not objective about their own performance. Second, people often do not know how decisions are being made.

As to the first of these problems, people usually consider their own work either outstanding or, at a minimum, above average. Some even play little entrapment games with their supervisors by feigning a belief that they are "only" above average, while expecting the supervisor to contradict them by stating that they are too modest and are in fact outstanding. Few individuals rank their own work as average, almost none as below average or unsatisfactory. There are very good reasons for this phenomenon.

The ability of individuals to rationalize—to make facts seem to fit perceptions or conclusions already reached—is almost limitless. For individual workers, rationalization leads to the conclusion that their work is indeed better than average. If it can be demonstrated that this is not so, there is always the fallback position that their work would be better except for conditions outside their own control—the schedule, working conditions, the intransigence of the supervisor, etc. In other words, it is not their fault.

Obviously, by definition, everyone cannot be above average. If the word "average" is to have any significance, it marks a midpoint, and performance from within the group falls equally to the left and right of the midpoint. However, supervisors, in evaluating subordinates' performances, play along with this game, in part because they want to be nice and in part because it is easier to do so. In most rating patterns for libraries as for other organizations, as many as 80% of the rated group are ranked either outstanding or above average, and some of the "above average" individuals are offended at the "slight." This accommodation might at first seem harmless, but it affects the implementation of salary policy. Employees rated as "above average" find that they receive salary increases that are average or even below average. At this point it is too late to tell them that the performance evaluation was exaggerated.

Given the high level of expectations generated by lavish performance evaluations and their deflation by actual salary awards, it is little wonder that salary rarely acts as a motivator for further effort, and rarely is perceived as adequate reward for work already accomplished. Salary policy has developed into at best a neutral and at worst a negative motivational factor. The small amounts of money actually available are only part of the problem, because in any case expectations will outstrip delivery.

As mentioned above, the second reason for dissatisfaction with the merit pay system is that people often do not know what is being judged or how that judgment is made. In the absence of such understanding, they may indeed prefer an across-the-board approach, which at least they can understand. ("If salary increases are to be inadequate, then at least they must be inadequate for everyone and not just for me.") Misery does not just love company, it *insists* on it.

Proper performance evaluation must of course be based on job descriptions. These are poorly written in most libraries, but that is not by preference of their staff members. Most individuals would like to know what their jobs are and what levels of performance are expected. In many cases they never find out, except by inference through the salary award notification. Job descriptions, in turn, must be based on the goals, objectives and programs of the parent institution, and of course for libraries that is frequently the most direct problem. Goals are vague, and objectives are absent or unrealistic. Job descriptions that do not address the focus of organizational activities accomplish little.

Criteria for Salary Determinations

Salary decisions must be based both on the complexity of the work and on how well it is performed in accordance with standards *for that position.* The issues are related. If a senior reference librarian has a more demanding job description than a junior reference librarian (with pay scales to match), then it should be assumed that a senior librarian would be expected to perform to higher standards than his or her junior colleague. Their performance cannot be compared to one another, but rather to the standards of the job description. Indeed, the senior staff member would have to perform better to be given as high a rating as the junior person. It is one of the grave shortcomings of the performance evaluation process as practiced in many libraries that performance expectations do not change as appointment levels change, and senior staff members therefore receive higher evaluations than their junior colleagues, in effect being rewarded anew for rewards already achieved. This is a practice common in the academic setting, and it has been transferred to other environments. A full professor is already rewarded for being more than an assistant professor or associate professor. To be as "satisfactory," what more should a full professor, or a senior systems librarian, be expected to do?

In addition to the evaluation of performance, which should be reviewed and confirmed annually or semiannually, salaries are also based on the evaluation of the job itself. This job evaluation usually determines salary ranges for specific positions and should be a major factor in the establishment of starting salaries. In the evaluation of jobs as part of the wage and salary process, library positions differ little in character from those in other units. Some library managers argue that standard evaluation criteria do not apply to libraries. Wage and salary analysts are understandably skeptical.

Job Ratings

Jobs are normally evaluated by rating characteristics in a number of categories. Each characteristic is assigned a point value, and the point totals then determine the dollar value of the job. Salary analysts maintain that this process permits them to deal equitably with totally disparate jobs. In principle, at least, they are probably correct.

The most significant factors in the evaluation of a position are:

1) Education required;

2) Experience required;

3) Complexity of duties;

4) Supervisory responsibilities exercised;

5) Supervision received;

6) Level of people with whom the individual will interact;

7) Impact of error;

8) Unusualness or dangerousness of working conditions.

The first five of these categories carry the major weight in determining the salary value of a particular job. Of less significance, particularly in libraries, are the final three. The third and sixth points are self-explanatory. The others are discussed below.

As to education, the first question for the library supervisor to ask is whether the position requires an MLS. Does it require a subject masters degree as well? It is obviously to the advantage of the manager to have educational needs recognized, but it is equally important not to require more than the job warrants. Requiring excess education can force the manager into searching for—and paying for—characteristics that are really not needed.

When setting experience criteria, it is important to differentiate experience from mere time on the job. Experience is assumed to contribute to a cumulative learning process, in which additional skills or perspectives are gained. Simply doing the same things over and over, without learning anything new, is not enriching experience. It is also common to develop equivalencies between experience and formal educational requirements. This practice has become particularly prevalent in meeting equal employment and affirmative action guidelines. The general rule of thumb, at least in industrial wage analysis, is to equate two years of genuine experience with one year of education, although the Federal Office of Personnel Management applies one year of experience for one year of education. Such an approach must be followed with caution. Experience frequently develops skills without contributing an understanding of underlying principles.

As has already been noted, individuals may be rewarded excessively for the responsibility of supervising the work of others. At the same time, it can be argued that such a recognition is only fair, because the individual who directs the work of others has a far greater impact than one who is responsible only for what he or she can personally accomplish.

The supervision a position receives is in a sense also valid as an analysis category. Individuals who have more freedom and flexibility in performing complex duties and making judgments should be rewarded accordingly.

The impact of errors made in different kinds of jobs varies widely. Errors in some lines of work (train engineer, air traffic controllers) have far more serious consequences than in others. In this regard, it is difficult for librarians to make a particularly strong case for higher salaries.

Unusual and dangerous job conditions are also criteria for high salaries. Again, it is not likely that librarians can make much of a case when compared to coal miners or to those whose work requires heavy traveling and considerable unscheduled overtime.

From all these calculations a salary range will emerge, and each position will fit into a slot. It is likely that totally disparate posts in the same library will have the same salary range. Also, the ranges used in the library will probably be in effect for other units within the parent organization. In general, the library is better served through this formal process than through some municipal government personnel officer's uninformed perception of what librarians ought to be paid.

SALARY RANGES

Salary ranges invariably have minimums. Many, although not all, have maximums. Even those that do not have maximums have intuitive limits above which salaries are set only with a great deal of discomfort. Some organizations publicize their salary ranges. For some of these, such as the Federal Civil Service, specific steps are indicated (e.g., within a grade 7 position there is a very specific salary range, another for grade 5, etc.). Over the past several decades, as civil service ratings at the bottom and in the middle have grown more rapidly in response to political pressures and the maximums have remained capped, these ranges have lost much of their usefulness and flexibility. Even in organizations in which salary ranges are not made public, supervisors should be prepared to explain and defend them, because they become public knowledge in any case.

It is important for individuals to know not only how much they will be paid for their first day of work but also what their potential earnings in a specific job are. As individuals approach the salary ceilings for their particular posts, their salary increase potential is greatly limited unless they are qualified for promotion to a position with a higher salary range. Therefore, it is generally desirable to hire at or near the bottom of the salary range for the position, and rarely if ever above the midpoint. Hiring above the midpoint is unfair to the candidate, particularly if he or she does not even know the range. If a candidate cannot be enticed at a salary comfortably within the salary range for the position, it is probably better to look at other applicants.

AVOIDING UNFAIRNESS

Salary increases are usually calculated as percentages rather than as dollars, although the application of dollars is probably fairer, because it avoids the further widening of salary differentials referred to earlier. Even in union contracts and other egalitarian approaches, percentages are used.

To avoid inadvertent salary inequities, it is useful to rank order both salaries and performance evaluations of comparable subordinates. If the rank listings do not match, the problem becomes obvious. It becomes apparent who is grossly underpaid and who may be overpaid, at least in relation to fellow workers. These problems usually cannot be resolved immediately, but the supervisor can work toward a solution by granting larger or smaller increases to narrow the gap and ultimately eliminate it. If this is not done, and particularly if employees receive the same percentage increase, the gap will continue to widen.

In summary, salary policy is a method for reward, for encouragement, and if necessary, for punishment. For those subordinates who have job security it may be the most effective or even the only tool available to the supervisor. Organizations frequently have constraints that limit the supervisor's flexibility. Some of these constraints are legitimately imposed to avoid arbitrary actions. Others result from the attractiveness of egalitarianism. Supervisors who do have discretionary authority in salary administration and who fail to avail themselves of the opportunity are wasting their chance to communicate satisfaction with the employee's performance or lack of it.

11

Communication Today and Beyond

COMMUNICATION AND DECISIONS

The reader will already have noted, from earlier chapters of this book, that communication shortcomings lie at the root of the great majority of management problems. It is not usually their actions or decisions that get managers into difficulty with staff members. It is a failure to explain, a failure to specify intent and a failure to convince others that decisions have been carefully thought out. In part the importance of the communication process results from that special characteristic of human beings mentioned earlier in this work. It is not enough for us to be told *what,* we must also be told *why*—at least if we are expected to cooperate with the successful implementation of the decision.

It must also be remembered that an individual's ability to make facts seem to fit preferences and conclusions already established is almost infinite. If we are given any flexibility, we hear what we want to hear and we interpret what we have heard to mean what we would like it to mean. Much communication in personnel administration is complex, and consists of a mixture of praise and criticism. There are few listeners who accept both of these components in the exact balance in which they were intended.

Some management styles are more susceptible to communication problems than others. In general, the more direct or autocratic the decision, the greater the need to explain in order to avoid resentment.

In a style of decision making based on the reaching of consensus, the pressure for other communication mechanisms is lessened, because the very seeking of consensus is an ongoing communication process. It is generally assumed by many sociologist/management writers that policy determination through consensus is the most preferred approach. It is certainly the smoothest and calmest, but not necessarily the most appropriate, particularly in a library setting. It should be obvious that the seeking of consensus is a time-consuming process, and because it takes up the time of many individuals it is also expensive. Not all decisions can wait for a consensus to form. In addition, particularly in libraries, there tends to be a concentration of individuals not given to risk taking, and sometimes lacking in imagination. The process of reaching decisions by consensus tends to result in "safe" decisions, in progress through small incremental steps and in a lessening of innovation. That is the nature of decisions reached through compromise and averaging. However, if a form of consensus is achieved through the eloquence or forcefulness of one individual or a small group, then what results is really not consensus but manipulation.

The reaching of decisions through voting has some of the same characteristics as consensus, although it tends to be more rapid and it does have a mechanism for dealing with dissent by a minority. The difficulty for the supervisor, as noted earlier, may come in his or her inability to accept from a management standpoint the decision reached by the group. The supervisor may consider the decision impractical, irrelevant to the problem (if for example it requires additional funds known to be unavailable) or unacceptable to higher management.

It is when individuals have participated in what they were told was a consensus or democratic participatory process, only to find out that their decisions will not be implemented, that anger and resentment become paramount. This is a prime example of a failure in communication. If subordinates "assumed" a level of participation which was not intended, the wrong message was sent with disastrous results. If the supervisor "assumed" that the consensus or participatory decision would match the one he or she had already reached and that it would therefore be possible to claim a democratic style without having to practice it, the supervisor may be in for an unpleasant surprise, and be forced either to implement a decision considered inappropriate or overrule a decision which was invited.

The most generally effective style for management decisions in library settings is "consultative management," a process which relies heavily on effective communication. Properly practiced, it gives the manager access to subordinate's ideas and suggestions which are freely offered without misunderstanding or fear of reprisal. It retains for the manager the ability to make ultimate decisions, something for which managers are both responsible and also presumably paid. It does place on the manager the heavy responsibility of communication—initially when the ground rules under which information is being sought are established, and finally when the decisions reached, which may not match all or any of the solicited advice, are communicated. It is at that point that supervisors are obligated to explain why they decided as they did. Managers who reach their decisions more autocratically have an even greater need to communicate, to explain what they have done and why.

Communication in libraries as in other organizations flows in several directions, down from the supervisor, up from the subordinates, or horizontally either from within the group or from outsiders such as vendors, service organizations and library users. All of these forms of communication are important, but they have very different characteristics.

In general, downward communication in the promulgation of rules or instructions can always take place, although explanations may be lacking. Upward communication must be nurtured, because employees offer advice and suggestions at considerable risk if they perceive that management disagreement will bring about resentment or punishment. That perception may be incorrect, but if it is commonly held it will be just as binding. Intragroup communication is subject to a number of factors, including jealousies and rivalries, conflicts over authority and the fear that good ideas are stolen if freely divulged. Supervisors who ignore these undercurrents of human behavior live in a fool's paradise. Appeals that "everyone pitch in for the good of the organization" are never challenged, but there is a wide range of views concerning what that organizational good is. Invariably, that view also matches what the individual sees as best for himself or herself.

Communication comes in two broad basic types—oral and written. Both are important, and in many instances both are necessary to deal with particular issues and problems. It is important to stress this, because it has become fashionable to downgrade written communication as bureaucratic and restrictive. Library managers who fall prey to such emotional reactions are headed for a considerable amount of trouble.

ORAL COMMUNICATION

Oral communication is important for its immediacy and its informality. On an individual basis, it permits correction of mistakes and reprimands without creation of a barrier of resentment and defensiveness. Much oral communication is spontaneous and unplanned, and it is important that communication flow take place, particularly between supervisors and subordinates. Supervisors who always work behind closed doors, who never take a coffee break with the group, and who never make themselves casually available in the workplace lose much of that potential for informality, a process which can head off far more serious communication needs at a later time.

Oral communication is also an important ingredient of group meetings and "rap" sessions. The effectiveness of both of these situations is greatly exaggerated, and the considerable cost is rarely considered. Meetings become expensive because the attempt at democratization tends to make attendance much larger than necessary. Individuals are included who really have no interest in the agenda and nothing to contribute because we fear that they will resent being excluded. That fear is probably valid. ("If most of my colleagues, or rivals, are going to attend a meeting, I want to be there, too. I may complain later that the meeting was a waste of time. However, were I not there, I would suspect that matters of great importance affecting me directly had been discussed.") The need for the communication of facts to dispel rumors, even when the facts are unpleasant, has already been discussed. This is essential because no matter how disagreeable the facts, the rumors will be far worse.

Meetings

Because those in charge try to avoid the appearance of heavy-handed autocracy in controlling a meeting, discussions tend to run on endlessly and pointlessly. Few supervisors know how to chair a meeting, and there is a general perception that the use of parliamentary procedures in such settings is too bureaucratic and formal. That may be, but it is also true that the Parkinsonian principle that time spent on a problem is inversely proportional to its importance is validated in almost every meeting which lacks proper controls. This is true because trivial issues are both easier and safer to talk about.

Experienced managers know that meeting agendas, unless rigidly structured, will tend to run on until they run into a natural barrier. Two such barriers apply in any organization—lunch and the end of the working day. Open-ended meetings that begin at 9:00 a.m. will usually last until noon and will accomplish in three hours just about the same amount as a meeting started at 11:00 a.m. Meetings started at 4:00 p.m. will also finish expeditously.

The cost of meetings is not trivial. Twenty individuals with average salaries of $25,000 per year who spend three hours in a meeting will have cost the library some $750 in direct salaries alone, not including fringe costs or the lost time of unsupervised subordinates. If the meeting is held weekly, the annual cost can surpass $37,500.

At the same time, it is a mistake to assume that individuals enjoy attending these meetings. They insist on being there both because of a perceived sense of status in attending with their peers, and because they are afraid that if they are absent, something might happen to affect them. However, they resent the time wasted, and they feel no sense of participation from the cosmetic use of the committee process. Almost by definition, large meetings can accomplish very little. Small groups selected for the specific expertise of the members and given a very specific and limited charter can accomplish a great deal and also give the members an opportunity to feel good about it.

One-to-one meetings are essential in a management relationship, but they rarely take place, in part because of a cost-accounting approach to the communication process. Supervisors feel almost instinctively that it is wasteful to meet with one individual when they could be meeting with four or five at the same time. Probably the most consistent shortcoming of managers is their unwillingness or inability to "find" the time to meet with their subordinates on a one-to-one informal basis. This problem will be addressed later in this chapter in the context of the librarian's need to communicate with non-librarian superiors. It is clear that one-to-one meetings can only be effective if all subordinates are entitled to them. Some supervisors will insist that they do not have enough time for this process, but that claim is nonsensical. Finding one hour every two weeks for each of eight subordinates still only takes up 10% of the presumed work time, for what is clearly the most important and potentially the most effective function. Most supervisors waste far more time than that in tasks which could be performed by subordinates, or which are totally unnecessary.

In contrast to one-to-one meetings, the committee process ideally serves only downward communication. It is an effective setting for the boss to explain what is going to happen, what changes have been made, and what problems must be faced.

Strengths and Weaknesses of Oral Communication

The oral communication process has clear advantages, but it also has pitfalls in that oral communications can be misunderstood, forgotten and subject to differing interpretations. An oral communication cannot be documented. One person may insist something was said and the other may deny it.

Oral communication is essential in one area in which it is not used nearly enough, for the preliminary communication of ideas. This type of communication ideally takes place between two individuals, perhaps colleagues, but more often supervisor and subordinate. The environment is conducive to discussion and exploration because it is not threatening. Nothing has been written down, ideas can be modified without threatening the pride of authorship, and if a subordinate's suggestion really runs into an unexpected wall of opposition it can be gracefully withdrawn without permanent damage.

WRITTEN COMMUNICATION

Written communications are also essential, and it is useful to consider them as adjuncts to the oral communication process. Written communications are poor vehicles for the introduction of new ideas, particularly radical ones. This is because new ideas are threatening for most individuals and there is a tendency to look for reasons why they will not work. The manager may plausibly react as follows: "After all, if the idea were good, wouldn't I have thought of it myself?" Given the predisposition to find fault with new ideas and suggestions, the process of submitting them initially in written form provides plenty of opportunity for the individual inclined to reject. Once that decision has been made, the reasons for the rejection can be found.

Written communication does serve as the ideal vehicle for the confirmation of decisions reached in informal discussions. These results must be documented in written form, to avoid the dangers of forgetfulness or misinterpretation. The confirming memorandum for an oral agreement is usually written by the lower-level participant, who also has the most at stake in establishing the validity of a decision which has just been made. Confirming memoranda have almost the force of a contract. Unless a disclaimer is made, and also in written form, the initial interpretation stands. In confirming communications, as opposed to those that communicate new ideas, the burden is on the recipient. If they are not read, they become validated by default.

Written communications are also necessary to spell out organizational rules and policies, specific work instructions and job descriptions. The ability to misunderstand verbal instructions is almost infinite. Speakers tend to be indirect in particular when direct communication conveys unpleasant news or criticism, and there is the understandable human tendency to try to put things as pleasantly as possible. When this characteristic is added to the penchant of listeners to hear what they want to hear and to interpret it as they prefer to interpret it, misunderstanding becomes almost inevitable.

Written communication is also essential in the performance evaluation process. It is required in the development of job descriptions and performance expectations, which may evolve from a series of less formal discussions and exchanges of views. It is essential in the articulation of goals, objectives and program plans and strategies to which individual performance is related, so that subordinates can absorb and stress larger organizational objectives in performing their own jobs.

Written communication is also important in documenting the results of performance evaluation. This is particularly significant in dealing with a problem employee for whom disciplinary action may be contemplated. That is not to suggest that written performance evaluations, whether they contain praise, criticisms or dire warnings, should be a shock or a surprise for the recipient. As with the submission of new ideas and suggestions, they are confirming communications which establish in writing what both the originator and the recipient already know.

Formal writings are sometimes characterized as bureaucratic red tape. These smear words should not deter the diligent memorandum writer who knows when written communication is called for.

Formal written communications need not be hard to read. They should consist of simple declarative sentences that specifically address their subject. If the communication must exceed two or three pages, an executive summary of one or two paragraphs is useful.

VERTICAL COMMUNICATIONS

The literature of personnel administration is full of suggested techniques to enable the supervisor to find out what the subordinate is doing. The literature is generally silent on suggestions to subordinates on how to get supervisors to take an interest in this information. It is assumed that the supervisor who recognizes his or her own responsibility for monitoring the performance of subordinates need not be convinced of the importance of spending the necessary time to develop and use mechanisms for accomplishing this.

In libraries, though, this may be a real problem. While librarians may report to other librarian supervisors who can be expected to have both an interest in and understanding of what they do, ultimately the management chain leaves the library. Without exception, libraries in the final analysis report to non-librarians, be these managers in corporations, city managers or mayors or elected library boards, or senior academic officials in a university. In many cases these individuals have a less than clear understanding of what constitutes good or poor library performance, and in many cases they do not care.

There are a number of reasons for both the failure to understand and the failure to care. First, as already stated earlier in this book, libraries tend to lack specific and quantifiable performance targets for which success or failure can be measured. They may report size of holdings or circulation totals, but they do so without any framework which explains the difference between success or failure. Holdings and circulation statistics are poor targets in any case, both because ultimately they can be stretched to become unachievable, and because they have never been related to more specific and directly applicable results.

Second, non-librarian managers to whom libraries report have never been given a framework in which to consider the library's success or failure in specific programs as their own success or failure. Without that personal commitment, these managers tend to retreat to an evaluation process which assesses the library in terms of reactions from library users. These in turn are not very helpful, in part because they have been conditioned by prior service or the lack of prior service. In academia they tend to focus on collection size as the only significant criterion for evaluation.

Librarians who fail to catch the attention of their non-librarian managers are not the beneficiaries of trust and confidence, they are the victims of disinterest and detachment. These attitudes might be acceptable, even if insulting, if the library's personnel had sufficient authority to make all necessary commitments of policy and expenditure and to resolve all disputes to the library's satisfaction. Of course, this is never the case. Libraries therefore need the interest of their non-librarian supervisors because they need support and endorsement in the struggle for resources and in the resolution of disputes with other organizations. The function of the supervisor, it must be recalled, is not simply to monitor and control. It is also to facilitate and assist. Managers who do not perform these functions are only doing part of their job.

Getting non-librarian managers to be involved requires a variety of sometimes delicate strategies. Getting them to care requires a combination of rewards for support and punishment for lack of support. Ultimately, the upper-level manager must receive his or her share of credit for accomplishments and of blame for failures, particularly as these are caused by a lack of support.

Accomplishing this requires first of all the conveying of the message. This is not easily accomplished if the upper-level manager is difficult to reach or sees to it that he is. Librarians need individual face-to-face meetings with their non-librarian bosses, probably at least one hour every other week. In these meetings informal communication must occur, but it must be oriented to the presentation and discussion of specific proposals, leading ultimately to agreement and a confirming memorandum. Alternatives must be explored, and the implications both for the library and for the supervisor must be clearly understood in the framework of reward and punishment which applies in upward as well as downward management communication.

A decade ago a large number of academic libraries underwent an intensive self-examination of their own objectives and procedures under a program called Management Review and Analysis Program (MRAP). It was a useful and positive exercise, not only because it forced libraries to face the identification of problems and ranking of priorities, but also because it involved the library staff in that process, and thereby created a great deal of positive goodwill. As far as the MRAP process went, it can be considered a success, and after 10 years it could well be repeated.

However, MRAP stopped short of its greatest potential, because in the vast majority of instances the identification of problems and proposed solutions was never shared with faculty within the institution or with the academic administrators who control resources and therefore control future actions. If MRAP findings and recommendations had been presented to academic administrators, this presentation should have been within the framework of the following two points: 1) Do you agree with this report and its recommendations? If you disagree with any part of it, how would you alter it? and 2) How do you propose to participate in the implementation of what is now a set of objectives but can easily be a plan, either as the library has proposed it or as you have modified it?

In dealing with managers above as well as within the library, getting those who are in charge to accept the need for taking responsibility is often the greatest roadblock. It is largely the control of resources that dictates the decision process, or as it has been stated facetiously, "One statement of the golden rule is that those with the gold make the rules." Administrators who control resources also control priorities. It is easy enough to take credit for what is being supported. For the library administrator it is even more important that those in control also take responsibility (or blame) for the things they are not supporting, and for the things that are not going to happen. Lack of funds is the invariable excuse, but it is also a transparent one. In any organization setting there are sufficient funds for plans considered really important enough to implement.

Two other points are worth remembering. In communicating with outside superiors, management must avoid terminology that non-librarians do not understand because it is specific to the field. This communication must also focus on what is important to the larger organization, and not just to the internal workings of the library. Processing backlogs, for example, only have significance for the non-librarian supervisor when they inhibit utilization of material by library users or impact on other programs of information flow.

In management communication, particularly at upper levels, the dangers of being repetitive and unimaginative must be avoided. Peter Drucker's injunction is worth remembering: Managers never get credit for simply continuing to do a satisfactory job. That is assumed. They get credit only for innovation and for marketing.

12

Present and Future Issues for Library Managers

In libraries—as in business—personnel management is becoming an increasingly complex task. More and more managers are now required to cope with a growing number of personnel issues arising from an organizational environment that is being rapidly transformed by technology and other factors. The shifting focus of unionization efforts, the changing roles of information professionals and the integration of now separate library functions are just some of the issues that astute library managers will want to become familiar with, in order to anticipate what influence they will have on the day-to-day operations of the library.

THE DEVELOPMENT OF UNIONS IN WHITE-COLLAR SECTORS

One topic not previously dealt with in this book is what impact unions will have on libraries and librarians in the near future. The 1970s and 1980s have seen the acceleration of a trend to unionize all white-collar employees, which therefore includes not only library clerks but also professional librarians. In part this has been spurred on by office automation, in part by growing individual employee fear and uncertainty about an unprotected future. For these reasons, it may be helpful to examine the background of this movement and its significance for libraries.

Unionization in the United States and other western industrial nations developed from the recognition of the real inequities created by the industrial revolution. Unions were designed to provide:

1) greater bargaining power for salaries and wages;

2) a voice for the airing of complaints and grievances;

3) a mechanism for fairness and uniformity of treatment, and an end to favoritism and discrimination;

4) a social environment of togetherness for a common purpose; and

5) an outlet to permit advancement for individuals who considered themselves blocked by arbitrary constraints.

After a lengthy period of often bloody conflict, unions grew rapidly in the U.S. between 1935 and the early 1950s, with almost all that growth concentrated in factories and other blue-collar settings. The growth of unions was undoubtedly aided by legislation favorable to their formation passed by Congress during the administration of Franklin Roosevelt.

Since the 1950s the growth of unions in the industrial sector has fallen off sharply. Rather, the emphasis in unionization activities has shifted during the last 25 years to the public sector, and to clerical and white-collar employees. In all probability, the most dramatic growth has been in the almost complete unionization of public school teachers.

This represents a significant change. White-collar and professional employees, certainly including librarians, initially rejected all concepts of unionization. They felt "above" such activities, identified with management in labor-management disputes and felt they did not need unionization. Unlike industrial workers, these employees felt they had job security, promotion opportunities and at least relatively good pay.

The change in emphasis from factory to office unionization can be attributed to a number of factors. Employers gained a greater awareness and sensitivity in industry, and looked for ways to head off unionization. Some of the tactics were heavy-handed and involved moving factories from the heavily unionized Northeast to the largely non-unionized South, while other approaches showed a greater discernment. Employers sought to defuse the arguments of union organizers by providing directly those things which unions sought to provide—higher pay, promotion opportunities, job security, pleasant working conditions and attractive fringe benefits.

Organizations such as IBM established a posture that such enlightened management tactics were far preferable and in the long run cheaper than the threat of unionization. Other employers followed, and by the mid-1970s the activities of unions in industry had begun to decline, a decline that continues to this day. Added to this phenomenon was the continued transfer of jobs from the industrial to the office environment, as mechanization became more prevalent, as U.S. factory work was lost to overseas competition and as service industries grew at a rapid rate.

It was therefore logical for unions to look at clerical and professional employees as a source of new converts. At the same time, their efforts were assisted by the almost blind insensitivity of employers of white-collar workers to the concerns of their employees and to the attractions of unionization.

Libraries and Unions

Library employees and other professionals quickly found that their salaries were not growing as rapidly as those of skilled and even unskilled workers. In many municipalities sanitation workers were more highly paid than teachers or librarians, and the fact that this first group was unionized could not be ignored. Professional librarians and teachers found, for perhaps the first time, that they were not immune from layoffs and terminations, and that they no longer had the lifelong job security they had taken for granted. Cuts in government agency budgets, a decline in school-age populations and a shift in priorities to other programs were all taking their toll.

Increasingly, professionals are forming the new recruits to the union movement. In many cases, they still join reluctantly. To some extent, feelings of superiority may still remain. To a probably greater extent, they recognize that unionization carries with it a need for discipline and conformity every bit as great as that of the most bureaucratically structured organization. While some unions, like some libraries and other organizations, function more democratically than others, at times the need remains for an absolute commitment to the will of the majority or of the leadership.

In some instances, unions in professional organizations have been able to provide greater salaries and benefits. In others, this has not been the case. The evidence is inconclusive and at times contradictory. What unions have been able to provide is a greater consistency of policy and of its applications. Procedures for hiring, for salary increases, for layoffs and terminations and in many instances for promotion follow rigid and clearly understood rules. Since the approach is egalitarian, what results may or may not be of benefit to the individual.

However, to a considerable extent, librarians and other professionals have been willing to trade an existing system they did not trust and could not control for one in which they at least understood the rules, whether they liked them or not. This is yet another confirmation of the point made earlier that the most destructive element in any organization's dynamic structure is *uncertainty*. Beset by an absence of objectives that make sense or that are tied to available resources, and to an evaluation and salary system in which they consistently consider themselves undervalued, library employees have become very obvious candidates for unionization. Basically their management has almost literally forced them in that direction.

At the same time, there remain questions about the effectiveness of library unionization. The ultimate power of any union is in its willingness to strike, or—in environments in which strikes are technically forbidden—to engage in what are cynically called "sickouts" and "job actions." Workers who recognize that the public cannot dispense with their industry's services for any length of time can and do strike effectively. These include such sectors as transportation, the postal service and the coal industry. Police and firefighters can usually be successful in obtaining salary increases and other benefits greater than those of, for example, librarians, simply through the veiled hint of a possible strike, and a suggestion of the dire consequences.

Teachers have found the strike an effective tool, but librarians would be foolish to equate themselves with teachers in terms of public necessity. In addition to providing educational services, teachers also serve as what could be crudely termed baby-sitters. They provide a place to send the children, and this is increasingly important in households in which both parents work, or in single-parent families.

The threat of a librarian strike might not be as effective. Librarians who wish to avail themselves of unionization would do well to affiliate with a larger group with far broader economic power. In universities this might be a faculty union; for public libraries a group of municipal employees, perhaps including the police and sanitation workers. In universities, however, the rights of faculty unions as bargaining agents have recently been called into question. Court decisions in specific cases have determined that faculty, who control many of their working conditions, are already members of management and therefore not eligible for unionization. The issue is far from clear and may not be decided for many years.

Issues of professional library unionization, of the ultimate willingness of a professional librarian to deprive the public of his or her services as part of a power confrontation, are significant, but perhaps not as crucial as might be perceived.

Some organizations whose workers are not affiliated with unions might welcome their appearance, while others operate under personnel policies governing salary increases, hiring, promotion and termination which are indistinguishable from what would emerge from a union contract, with only salary levels left to be decided. Where managers have opted for this approach, it is not because of a commitment to fairness and the avoidance of favoritism that legitimatized early trade unionization, but because such ground rules make their job easier, simplify decision making and in many instances permit them to avoid decisions entirely by blaming everything on "policy." This author has already made it abundantly clear that he has no patience with managers who refuse to do what they are paid to do—make difficult decisions.

The rate of formation of unions in libraries will depend in great part on the willingness of managers to avoid the creation of vacuums in which unionization flourishes.

PROSPECTS FOR THE FUTURE

It is unlikely that we will see as great a series of changes in the way people work as has been evident in the development of products and services made possible by technological innovation, which has had far-reaching consequences for virtually all industries. Individuals are still going to be constructed as they have been in the past and will be subject to the same motivations and fears. That does not mean that the majority of social scientists will not continue to examine the individual worker and try to figure out what makes him tick. However, if we can judge from past experience, the cumulative body of knowledge will not necessarily or automatically lead to more involved subordinates, to more sensitive and aware managers, to greater satisfaction or to higher productivity. We may have learned by now that sweeping generalizations and the search for quick-fix solutions do not work. Concepts of worker participation, job enrichment, quality circles, flextime and the four-day work week have all been introduced with considerable publicity and the promise of a breakthrough success. They have failed as generalizations as they have failed or succeeded in specific instances. New generations of motivational theories will meet the same fate.

This is true because workers, in libraries as in other settings, will continue to react and respond as the individuals they are and will forever continue to be. What is effective for one subordinate is ineffective or counterproductive for another. That will be as true in the future as in the past and present. Managers would be well advised to be aware of newly evolving concepts of personnel administration and to learn of their successes and failures, keeping in mind that successes are reported far more frequently than failures, and that some failures even masquerade as partial solutions. In considering the application of these techniques, all library managers should bear in mind the unique mix of personalities, ambitions, fears and hopes that constitute their work force, as well as the objectives and programs to which the library is committed.

SPECIFIC PREDICTIONS FOR LIBRARIES

With all of these caveats in mind, some general predictions can be risked:

1) There will indeed continue to be a substantial technological impact on the nature of the library profession. It will affect what individuals do, and the kinds of skills and personality traits required. To a great extent, the routine operations which characterize the public view of the library and the haven of some introverted workers will disappear, to be subsumed in national or international computer systems over which the individual library will have little if any control.

These functions will include filing of cards and other bibliographic records, circulation, overdue notices and the presently Byzantine process of generating an interlibrary loan request. The emphasis in libraries and information centers will be on the professional functions of information analysis, information intermediation and individualized problem solving. These functions in turn require skills and attitudes which some professional librarians already have, which some can acquire and for which some simply will not be adaptable at all.

Managers will have to deal with these questions individually and sensitively. There will be no easy answers, and for some problems no satisfactory answers at all. Differentiations between professional and clerical work will, in this setting, become much sharper. There will be fewer clerks because technology will absorb many of their jobs. For the remaining clerks motivational techniques may be more difficult because many if not most of the jobs will have little if any potential for advancement. Job satisfaction will have to be induced for a small but important job well done.

2) Librarians will be called on for greater accountability for their decisions, and for their expenditure of funds provided by outside organizations. To some extent this is already beginning to occur, to the great discomfort of some practitioners, but for these people things will get a lot worse rather than better. The concept of a library as a "self-evident good" is no longer affordable, as the library competes for funds with too many organizations which also consider themselves self-evidently good. In the for-profit sector librarians are expected to explain their contribution to cost-benefit, or at least to institutional cost-effectiveness. A similar requirement for public, academic and school library administrators will not be far behind.

3) Continuing rapid changes in technology and the rapidly evolving role of information professionals will bring librarians at all levels into contact with greater complexity. A continuing process of education and training for all library employees appears a foregone conclusion. For managers the recognition of this need must be incorporated into the development of budgets and work schedules. Continuing education is expensive and time-consuming, and perhaps the greatest expense is the loss of productive time.

Allowance for education and training must be built into organizational objectives and into plans for bringing them to fruition. When educational or training requirements come into conflict with backlogs, backlogs now usually win out, and this is particularly true in perpetually understaffed libraries. We still try to hide our problems from our patrons and sometimes even from the executives whose actions or inactions brought them about.

This attitude is one we cannot afford in the future. The need for continued learning also means the recruitment of individuals who can not only do more than perform the requirements of the present job, but who also have the potential for continued growth and the openness to adapt to changed circumstances. Factoring such requirements into job descriptions must be done carefully to avoid both the charge and reality of discriminatory tactics. At the same time, these personality requirements are very real and cannot be sidetracked.

4) Largely because of technology and the increasing complexities of the information-gathering process, libraries have already started to become totally integrated systems rather than separate compartments of functional specializations. This trend will continue and accelerate. The most important task for library professionals will be the interaction with fellow professionals both inside and outside the library setting. We will always have a need for some specially trained introverted humanist scholars; however, the greatest emphasis will be on people-oriented people, who can plan, interact, articulate and persuade.

In addition to the liberal arts background considered so generically important to library work, we will also need our share of technologically trained and business trained individuals. To attract these and the high-quality professionals we will need in all specializations, we must develop salary scales to make the work attractive and performance requirements to make it worthwhile.

5) In libraries as elsewhere there must be a growing recognition that individuals need to understand not only what they do, but why they do it and why their doing it well is important. This is of course the lesson of the Japanese system, which permits workers to concentrate on planning and executing their own jobs. This in turn encourages them to make suggestions to improve their own performance, and reinforces the knowledge that the contribution of even the lowest-level worker is important.

This ability to persuade the individual worker of his or her importance in the overall process is an activity we have traditionally performed quite poorly in the United States, and not only in libraries. Paternalism has sought to shield employees from the realities of the organizational setting on the false premise that they did not care or did not want to know. Traditionally confrontational management-labor interactions sought to construct a chasm between worker and manager, by insisting that workers were only responsible for doing what they were told and not for what happened as a result of that instruction.

We now begin to understand not only that this approach undermines productivity and quality concern, it also destroys morale and incentive. In libraries this means that all employees, down to the lowest level, must understand the objectives of the organization, the means for successfully achieving them and their own crucial role in that accomplishment. Before we can do any of these things, of course, we must develop the set of meaningful and achievable objectives that are so lacking in libraries.

It is possible that the implementation of this last requirement may be sidetracked by its confusion with other and quite separate issues—those of a drive for a greater participation or consensus in the decision process. As stated earlier in this book, such an approach toward democratization may be important for some workers and unimportant or even threatening for others. It may be consistent with the achievement of organizational objectives in some instances. In others it may lead either to failure of the effort or a reneging on promised levels of participation. Either of these results is disastrous.

Most workers do not insist on such a level of involvement, although it is more important for some than for others. Certainly, Japanese workers neither have it nor expect it. What all workers appear to want, and what they certainly seem reasonably entitled to have, is some input to the overall structuring of their own job, freedom in carrying it out and judgment by results rather than methods. ("Leave me alone, and tell me how I did.") They must understand why it matters that they do their work well, or for that matter that they do it at all, and must also understand the personal consequences of all of this. ("Reward me in accordance with what I did.") This approach outlines a far more generic and yet far safer approach to personnel management, because it allows for the individuality of each worker, and for the articulation of his or her own priorities for personal growth, authority, money, recognition, pleasant working conditions and a myriad of other factors.

In the final analysis, personnel administration will become, particularly in libraries where its appreciation and skillful application has lagged for such a long time, the crucial ingredient for successful organizational performance it should always have been. This will occur as we recognize that quick-fix solutions will not save us. We will only be rescued by the intelligence, ingenuity, sensitivity and courage of individual managers.

It behooves the profession of librarianship to concentrate on the development of these personnel management skills. They will be a fixed requirement even as the technical emphasis of the profession, the holdings of our libraries and the physical appearance of our buildings continue to change.

Personnel Problem Exercises

HOW TO USE THE EXERCISES

The approach recommended for use of the personnel problem exercises that follow involves deliberating a number of questions, based on sample day-to-day management situations which reflect a need for both analysis and anticipation. Glib, simplistic answers serve no useful purpose, no matter how eloquently presented, since complex problems often require complex solutions.

While it is clear how these exercises can be used effectively in a textbook or teaching context, their use by library managers may require some clarification. Basically, managers should approach these problems as an exercise in discipline. Many of us reach conclusions and then tailor these to specific problems. This tactic, however, has its drawbacks, and it is vital that we look at a given problem and identify a variety of alternatives, rather than allow ourselves to be ruled by preconceptions.

Interpersonal relationships as presented in these exercises are multifaceted. Every case has several participants, each with his or her own set of priorities and preconceptions. Problem exercises of this sort have more than one point of view, and the ultimate selection of a decision (because in such exercises as in real life an ultimate decision must be made) includes an assessment of both alternatives and risks.

These are the questions a manager should consider while reviewing each problem exercise:

1) What is the problem or are the problems with which the manager must deal? How did the problem arise? Could it have been avoided?

2) What are all of the alternative approaches for dealing with this problem? What are the pros and cons, the risks and benefits of each approach?

3) Which alternative do you plan to implement? When? How? Whom if anyone do you need to consult? Inform? Ask for permission?

4) What is your assessment of probability of success for your approach? What do you plan to do if it fails?

(Note: All these case studies are real, and based either on the writer's own experience or on a situation about which he has firsthand knowledge. Names, places and some details have been changed to protect anonymity.)

PROBLEM EXERCISE 1

Phyllis Robinson had been hired 18 months ago to bring the library of the Grover Chemical Co. "into the 20th century." It was a situation not uncommon in corporate decision processes. After many years in which the library had suffered from benign neglect, a new vice president for research had been appointed. He knew what other libraries and information centers were doing to provide information access through mechanization, and he wanted the gap closed as quickly as possible.

Phyllis, who had advanced degrees in chemistry and library science, and strong experience in the implementation and management of computerized information systems, had been immediately hired and encouraged to make rapid and sweeping changes. Money or the upgrading of staff had not been major concerns at the time. What the vice president wanted, he usually got.

It had been an exhilarating time. Moving rapidly as she knew she must, Phyllis had opted for acquiring proven combinations of computer hardware and software already developed by others. Five new professionals had been hired. Three of these were additional positions, two had been replacements for long-time employees. One of these had retired, the other had relocated with her husband. Phyllis did not mourn their departure, because the original staff had been hired with entirely different performance criteria in mind. Or, as Phyllis sometimes thought to herself, with no criteria of professional performance in mind.

The library users had been surprised and then enthusiastic about the changes being made. Instead of excuses, they were getting service. The library staff not only provided access to a variety of online information sources, but also undertook more complex information searches. They also had taken over control of internal reports and laboratory notebooks, which were now part of the computer-addressable file. The more the engineers and chemists in the company became aware of potential services, the more they wanted. That was all right, because corporate management had responded to justifications for additional equipment, additional material and additional staff, and presumably would continue to do so.

During all this time, Lillian Dawson floundered in the backwash. She had come to Grover 20 years ago, although she was now only 45. She had come straight from library school, and had not really planned on special library work, but it paid better than other opportunities. Lillian was bewildered and frightened by the changes taking place, and Phyllis felt sorry for her. Lillian had been appointed as a reference librarian when reference at Grover Chemical meant primarily borrowing articles and books through interlibrary loan, because the collection contained so little. She was totally incapable of functioning as a reference librarian in an age of online terminal access for both literature searching and circulation control.

Phyllis had offered Lillian a number of opportunities to attend library automation workshops and seminars, and to take university courses fully funded by the corporation. Lillian had declined when she could, pleading that her home activities kept her busy. When Phyllis insisted that Lillian attend certain seminars, she had gone but they had made no discernible difference in either her attitude or her work.

Lillian hated what had happened to her job and to the library, but she made no attempt to adapt and rebuffed what Phyllis felt were ample offers of assistance. And yet she would not leave, either. Phyllis could guess at the reason. Twenty years at Grover had put Lillian into a fairly high salary bracket, and there was certainly nothing of comparable pay elsewhere in the community.

For quite a while Phyllis had managed to work around the obstacles in both attitude and performance which Lillian Dawson presented. She had been able to hire additional staff, and funds had been plentiful. She had found other tasks for Lillian to perform, special projects and calculations that might prove useful. In truth, Phyllis Robinson thought they were probably really clerical tasks, but Lillian performed them satisfactorily and almost gratefully.

And then an expenditure ceiling went into effect. Grover Chemical Co. had suffered a disappointing financial year and the corporate president had declared a period of no further growth in either staff size or budget dollars. There was little the vice president for research could do in the face of such an order except counsel patience.

At the same time, Phyllis Robinson knew the flood of user expectations that she had created would not be stemmed quite so easily. The next year at least would require tougher and more efficient operations, and a staff that could adapt and mature to meet these challenges. And Phyllis felt that she could no longer afford the luxury of having Lillian Dawson on the staff.

PROBLEM EXERCISE 2

In six months the town of Oakmont would be celebrating the 200th anniversary of its founding, and the mayor had suggested that the public library mount a display of photographs, articles, clippings and other items to show the growth of the community. Angela Battaglia thought it an excellent opportunity to publicize the public library. The display would be prominently featured on the main floor of City Hall, and additional money for the cost of mounting the exhibit might be made available "as long as it wasn't exorbitant."

Angela knew that the library had boxes and boxes of just the right material. They were all stored in the basement and there was little information about what was in each one, but Angela knew that the reference staff was interested in local history and qualified to do the work. She had happily agreed to the mayor's request.

When she had convened her staff of three reference librarians, they had been equally enthusiastic. All sorts of ideas and suggestions came to the surface, and Angela felt a glow of satisfaction at the thought of this competent and professional staff she had assembled. To give them full rein, she had urged them to work independently or together, as they preferred, selecting potential exhibit material in their spare time over the next four months. She would then meet with them again so that the final determinations could be made, and two months would be adequate for the actual assembly.

When Angela met with her reference librarians again four months later, she was horrified to learn that absolutely nothing had been done. The reaction to her mounting anger had initially been one of offering excuses, but the mood quickly turned belligerent. They didn't see how they could have been expected to find the time for this major project when the library had just completed its busiest two months, and the two months before that hadn't been exactly quiet, either. Moreover, with the workloads they faced in the next several weeks, none of them felt that they could promise to find time for this extra project. They would try but that was all. If Angela wanted this done, they felt she should have told the mayor she needed to hire extra people on a temporary basis.

PROBLEM EXERCISE 3

Eleanor Marland knew from her 15 years of experience as a library director that the scheduling of vacations was potentially very troublesome. The Somerset Public Library granted two weeks' vacation to any employee who had started work before September 1 of the previous year. It took 10 years of service to qualify for a third week. Eleanor knew that other libraries had more generous policies, but this approach was consistent with that of other Somerset municipal agencies, and library employees knew and accepted it. There was a little occasional grumbling, but nothing serious.

Scheduling vacations was sometimes a more delicate matter. With a total staff of 14 including a professional staff of six, Eleanor did not feel that she could allow too many individuals to be gone at any one time. At most two clerks, and never more than one professional. Unfortunately, Eleanor had learned, people usually wanted to take their vacations at the same time. The most popular times were the first two weeks of July, when Independence Day allowed vacations to be stretched an extra day, and the period just before Labor Day, when the same thing occurred.

And so Eleanor had, very early in her administrative career, devised a policy which had worked well for her. Staff members were asked to put in their requests by February 15, and in case of conflicts seniority would decide. Those who later changed their minds would have to take pot luck. Everyone understood the policy, and everyone agreed it was fair, even those with little seniority.

The schedule had never caused any problems for Eleanor. She enjoyed skiing, and she took her vacation in early March. Everyone else preferred the summer for both personal and family reasons, Betty Tolliver had not been as lucky. A reference librarian with six years of service, Betty had always hopefully requested the first two weeks in July. Invariably, Alice Baker, who was also a reference librarian and who had been at the Somerset Library longer, also asked for those same weeks, to visit her sister. It was probably more out of habit than for any other reason, and Alice could probably have gone at a different time. However, Betty never complained, and simply rescheduled her vacation for later in the summer. Eleanor had never broached the question, because she did not believe in creating problems where there were none.

Then Alice had retired last August, and now Betty should be able to have her first choice. In fact, as Eleanor arranged the vacation request slips on her desk, she saw one minor clerical conflict, but nothing that would stop Betty from finally having her first two weeks in July. One slip was missing. Agnes Farmer, hired to replace the retiring Alice Baker in time to qualify for vacation, had not turned in a slip. Eleanor was about to walk over to Agnes' desk to remind her that, although she had last preference, she still ought to schedule her vacation, when Agnes walked into her office.

Seeing the vacation slips spread out on the desk, Agnes came straight to the issue. "I didn't fill out a vacation preference form because I didn't really see the point. My husband works for the Excelsior Corporation, and they always close the plant for two weeks each summer for vacation. I have to have mine during the first two weeks in July."

PROBLEM EXERCISE 4

"It isn't fair!" Alice Watson said to herself as she returned to her own office in the Technical Services Department at Webster State University. Alice had just had an unsettling meeting with Margaret Goodrich, the library director. There had been such meetings frequently in the two years since Margaret was brought in to direct the Webster Library and immediately started making unreasonable demands. John Franklin, now retired and living in Arizona, certainly wasn't like that. The six years after John had selected her for the post of Head of Technical Services had been happy ones. As a cataloger at Webster for more than 30 years before this assignment, Alice certainly knew what catalogers could or could not accomplish. John had accepted her expertise and advice. Margaret had come in with her own very fixed ideas. Not only did she have the university administration all stirred up about changing the library to what Margaret called a "modern information facility," but she had also brought some new staff members who shared her views into key administrative positions. Membership in OCLC was all right, Alice felt, but surely they had to understand that one couldn't simply open the doors to all of the errors in cataloging that other libraries made. OCLC data could be used under certain circumstances, but it had to be checked carefully, and sometimes it took longer to fix somebody else's mistakes than to do the work from scratch. She knew that, and her loyal staff knew that, too. Even the kids newly hired from library school quickly saw and accepted the need to maintain standards and procedures to safeguard the quality of the collection.

However, all Margaret seemed to be worried about was the cataloging backlog, and the past few meetings had been most unpleasant. Alice had to agree that the present backlog, which hovered at around 14 months, was high, but surely management ought to be able to understand that it took more staff to accomplish more, and her positions had been frozen at the same level as three years ago, before all these efforts to raise funds and acquire donated collections began. Obviously the backlog had risen, and it took all of her efforts, including lots of personal unpaid and unappreciated overtime, to have now stabilized it at its present level. On top of everything else, they wouldn't leave her alone to do her work. There were planning meetings, systems development committee meetings, personnel appraisal and sensitivity seminars. As if she didn't know how to supervise people!

This new requirement was the last straw. Margaret had informed her, with her usual smugness, that the library had just snagged the Boniface collection of more than 15,000 volumes dealing with the exploration of the early West. Probably not more than 10% of these books were already in the library, she guessed, because that emphasis on early American history was new to Webster, and the history faculty members specializing in that area had just been added.

Special publicity was planned, and it was very important that the entire Boniface collection be cataloged and incorporated into the library holdings within a year, when a ceremony commemorating the first white settlement in the state would be held.

A year! Alice still shuddered at the thought. Even assuming that 10% or even 15% of these books were duplicates (and it would take time to find that out), that was the equivalent of more than one-third of their normal annual productivity. And Margaret wanted this material cataloged together with the regular material, and without an increase in the backlog, because both the faculty and the reference librarians were already pretty unhappy at the time delays.

Margaret had made it clear that there would be no additional staff, no temporaries, no overtime, no additional money at all. In response to Alice's question as to how something was to be done with nothing, Margaret had answered that it was high time that the department looked at ways to streamline its procedures, and to make greater use of cooperative cataloging. Such an approach would allow them to absorb the Boniface collection this year, and to eliminate the backlog in the next two years. Margaret made it quite clear that was what she expected, and her attitude invited no further arguments.

"Well," Alice thought, "we shall see!" Margaret obviously knew nothing about cataloging and its complexities. All her experience was in public services and administration, and she considered herself a pro at developing automated systems. She had even brought in a couple of systems analysts, with money that could have been used to hire at least four more catalogers. Fortunately, Alice had been able to keep these systems people out of her department, because they were working on a new circulation and search system.

Alice clearly knew what she would have to do next. She would call a meeting of her professional staff, tell them what Margaret had just told her, and ask them for their reactions. She knew pretty well that those would be. After all, these were her people. However, it was important that Margaret Goodrich also hear from others how unreasonable her expectations were. Then Margaret would be forced to modify her simpleminded approach to all these problems. She'd have to give them more staff, allow them more time, or accept an even bigger backlog. Her loyal staff were, after all, human beings. They couldn't perform miracles.

PROBLEM EXERCISE 5

Hiring Armando Lopez eight years ago had been an extremely pleasant experience for Rita Merrivale, personnel librarian at Ivory University, and it had also given great satisfaction to Inez Fulton, the library director. The library, like other units of the university, was fully committed to affirmative action, but at the same time maintained its insistence on qualified candidates.

When the post of assistant business librarian had become vacant, Armando was a natural. He was an honors graduate from a prestigious library school with an undergraduate major in public administration. He had taken courses dealing with business literature and online searching, and he had the highest references from both his faculty members and his part-time supervisor at the business branch library at which he worked while attending school. Armando was personable and articulate, and he had been everybody's first choice.

Since coming to Ivory he had done nothing to disappoint these expectations. He had married shortly after he started his job, and was now the very proud father of two small girls. Despite these pressures, he had enrolled in the MBA program at Ivory, and had completed it on a part-time basis in four years. When the head business librarian retired two years ago, the search committee of librarians and business faculty members went through the process of a formal search, and had recommended Armando as the first choice. Both Rita and Inez had been delighted to concur.

At the age of 32 Armando Lopez was in charge of a major academic business library. He turned his vigorous energies to improving library service for his patrons and to professional activities in both the American Library Association and the Special Libraries Association. Inez occasionally discussed library professional personnel with the vice president of Academic Affairs, and Armando had been noted as an individual with considerable promise. Of course, Inez recognized that others, outside Ivory University, would also have noticed.

For this reason, but primarily because he deserved it, Armando Lopez had been treated as generously as salary policies and budgetary limitations allowed. He had achieved tenure without difficulty in his seventh year, together with promotion to Associate Librarian. It was normal to wait at least another seven years before proposing a further promotion to full librarian status, but Inez had already concluded that in this case the waiting period could be cut to five. Armando was, at this stage, the highest paid library staff member for his length of service, and one of the better paid branch heads. Rita and Inez were certain that nobody resented this, because he deserved it.

When Armando requested a meeting with Inez, she had some trepidations, and her fears were immediately confirmed. Armando began slowly and carefully, almost deferentially. He was happy in his assignment at Ivory, and he had been treated very fairly. He had no complaints whatsoever. He had not sought any other job offer. When Transpacific University contacted him about the vacant head business librarian position, he had almost declined outright. However, Transpacific was near the home of his wife's parents, and the timing coincided with a planned vacation trip. He saw no harm in at least visiting Transpacific since he would be in the area in any case.

The visit to Transpacific had impressed him positively, but he did not consider their library or its program superior to Ivory's. He considered them comparable, and in one sense his visit had confirmed his pleasure at being where he was. However, he could not ignore the offer he had just received. It was for the post of Business Librarian, with tenured full librarian status, and at a salary $8000 above his present salary, which included the increase he had just received two months ago.

He was in a quandary, and made it clear he did not know what to do. He was not issuing any ultimatums, because he felt he had no right to do so. His present salary at Ivory was fair, but an increase of $8000 was something he could not dismiss lightly. He had a young family, and there were certainly financial needs and pressures. Did Inez have any advice she could offer him?

Inez quickly reviewed university policy and tradition in her own mind. The university did occasionally match or partially meet outside salary offers for key faculty members from a discretionary fund at the disposal of the vice president, but had never done so or been asked to do so for librarians. If she asked the administration, there might be some support. Immediate promotion to full librarian would be more difficult, probably impossible, but this would not stand in the way of salary adjustment.

At the same time, Inez wondered if she should do anything at all. Armando was well paid at present—even he agreed with that. Nor had he insisted on a particular increase, on the threat of leaving. Still, she was pretty sure that if she did nothing, he would accept the Transpacific offer, and she couldn't really blame him.

PROBLEM EXERCISE 6

Norma Blodgett had been a clerk at the Millvale Public Library for the last nine years, since the youngest of her children started school and she decided to return to the work force. Her bachelor's degree in English literature had been earned 18 years ago, and didn't seem to qualify her for any more remunerative jobs in Millvale. Besides, as she pointed out whenever the subject came up, Norma liked and had always frequented libraries.

The library, for its part, was delighted to have her. Although Norma's normal duties involved circulation and general public assistance, she willingly took a crack at reference questions whenever these came up and others were busy. With an increase in library hours not matched by an increase in staff, that happened more and more frequently. Edna Hellman, who was Head of Reference, felt no particular concern when this occurred. Norma did as good a job as any of the reference librarians, she knew the collection and from observing others she had learned the techniques of the reference interview and the tactics for obtaining information from outside sources. Edna was quite sure that virtually all of the library patrons simply assumed that Norma was a professional.

Edna felt vaguely uneasy that the library was taking advantage of Norma's skills and good nature without paying for them, but Norma didn't seem to mind and never complained. Millvale municipal government salary policies permitted few deviations from across-the-board annual increases, although once, three years ago, Edna had been able to justify a special merit increment. Norma accepted this gratefully.

Since Edna knew that one of the regular reference librarians would be resigning in May, she decided to promote Norma to the new vacancy when it occurred. She knew that none of the staff members would have any objection to this promotion, and she informed the library director, who concurred with her recommendation. She then felt safe in imparting the good news to Norma, who was both pleased and grateful. When the paperwork promoting Norma reached the City Manager's office it was returned unapproved. Norma was qualified for the promotion, but she also had to be the best qualified available candidate, as municipal civil service procedures specified. The position had to be advertised; only then could a decision be made and justified.

When the job of junior reference librarian was advertised and posted in the library, it brought applications from three current library school students who would be graduating in May. All had strong recommendations and had taken advanced courses in reference. It also yielded an application from a professional librarian with six years of reference experience who would be moving to Millvale next month. Finally, and most surprisingly, it triggered an application for lateral transfer from Sally Greene, who had been a competent cataloger for three years. When she was asked why she had applied for a position which paid no more, Sally answered that she preferred reference work to cataloging. "You know that I was a reference librarian in Iowa for three years before I came here." Edna didn't know, but was unwilling to admit it. She wasn't responsible for hiring catalogers.

In any case, Edna now faced a difficult problem. She still wanted to promote Norma, and Norma expected to be promoted. At the same time, Edna knew that the justification for her choice would be very difficult. Millvale Public has a staff of 18 professionals and 34 clerks, plus student and summer help. The Head of Reference and Head of Technical Services report to the Library Director. Because of the relatively small size of the staff, there had never been any need for a personnel officer and, in this case, the decision rested squarely on Edna's shoulders alone.

PROBLEM EXERCISE 7

Tom Montgomery definitely was not working out and something had to be done about it. The situation could no longer be ignored. Having decided that, library director Sally Marshall's orderly mind moved immediately to determine the cause.

In one sense, a major part of the blame was easy to assign, but that didn't really help. Frank Everhart, who had retired from the directorship last year, had to be given a major part of the responsibility, but how did that help her now?

His decision to employ a systems officer for the library was one she could not quarrel with. Had she found such a gap, she also would have moved to fill it. Although a major research institution with more than 3 million volumes in holdings, the university library still operated on the fringes of the Dark Ages when it came to library automation. Yes, they had OCLC access, but no computerized holdings lists, serials check-in procedures, COM catalogs, circulation records or materials usage analyses.

She could also not quarrel with Tom Montgomery's qualifications for the position. Tom was not a librarian, but his 10 years with IBM had made him thoroughly familiar with the characteristics and design of information systems. He had followed this with five more years as senior systems engineer with one of the major bibliographic utilities. Tom was knowledgeable about library automation, he was active in the Association of Computing Machinery and Data Processing Management Association, and competent in every way to lead the library's onslaught on the implementation of new technology.

Why, then, did he have trouble from almost the first day he had arrived three years ago? Perhaps there was resentment at his high salary, second only to first Frank's and now her own, but surely her staff members knew that qualified and competent systems people were expensive.

It was also true that Tom was direct and forceful in his communications. He was not a flatterer and he had little time for small talk or socializing. His behavior on the job was professional, his outside interests lay elsewhere. No, that wasn't it, either. If Tom were a little more ingratiating, it might have helped a little, but not much.

Sally had to conclude that the problem began with the very method of selecting Tom and then introducing him to the library staff. Frank had brought Tom into the library into a staff position reporting immediately to the director, and then told him as well as the staff that his responsibility would be to identify areas which could benefit from automation, and then to develop procedures for automating. Frank instructed all of the library departments to give Tom their full cooperation. He had also bragged, to staff members and to the chancellor, that he expected an individual with Tom's knowledge and experience to implement considerable labor-saving mechanisms which could reduce costs and even produce a surplus which could be transferred to the materials budget.

Immediately and instinctively the library staff had closed ranks against this outsider. They never openly opposed or confronted Tom; they simply never told him anything. When he asked for copies of memoranda he should have received, they apologetically sent him the specific item, then promptly left him off the next distribution list. Since Tom didn't even know what he should have been getting in the first place, he usually didn't know what to ask for. His requests for meetings were delayed and postponed. His requests for staff time for detailed discussions were deferred until "they had more time."

Two years after his arrival, Tom still had accomplished virtually nothing. When he had complained to Frank about the lack of cooperation, Frank had made one of his famous haranguing speeches at the weekly management review sessions, reminding everyone that he expected them to cooperate with Tom in his assignments. Everyone agreed that this was important and that coordination would improve as soon as the present crisis project was completed. And yet nothing happened. And then Frank retired.

Sally had now been here for six months, and up to now she had been able to rationalize that she had other more important immediate priorities. The new building design, the incipient chemistry faculty revolt and recruitment of several key subordinates were issues now safely in hand, and it was time to turn to Tom Montgomery.

Tom had spoken to her a couple of times about his frustrations. She had been sympathetic, and assured him that it was a concern to which she would address herself shortly. Sally supposed things could be worse. The faculty obviously didn't care that nothing had happened. Most of them probably preferred that. The chancellor had apparently mercifully forgotten, and the library staff was steadfast in its conspiracy of silence. It was almost as though Tom Montgomery did not exist, and that his chair at management meetings stood empty.

PROBLEM EXERCISE 8

Vicki Landrum's two years as an interlibrary loan clerk in the Foxworth University Library had been uneventful, and Marion Rogers was therefore surprised to learn from her secretary that Vicki had been in that morning and requested an immediate appointment. As head of the Reference Department, Marion had overall management responsibility for about 100 individuals, including professionals, clerks and an ever-changing sea of student faces.

She recalled Vicki as a pleasant and cheerful woman, perhaps thirty, whom she occasionally encountered in the supermarket, usually with two small children in tow. As she awaited Vicki's arrival, Marion felt uneasy. If I only had a clue as to what she wanted, Marion thought. Marion liked to be in control of situations and well-prepared for meetings, and she certainly didn't feel that way right now. Harriet Bogardus, Vicki's immediate supervisor, had just started her vacation, and whatever Vicki's problem was, she obviously felt it needed immediate attention.

In the few minutes remaining, Marion decided to review Vicki's file. It gave very little additional insight. Actually she'd worked here closer to three years, and her application form indicated her status as divorced with two children. Marion wondered if it was still legal to ask about that. If it was not, the administrators who ran Foxworth would probably be the last to know. A private university originally founded by the Methodist Church, but now nonsectarian, Foxworth's proud traditions and wealthy and loyal alumni were not necessarily matched by present academic achievement or modern thinking.

It wasn't a bad place to work. The salaries for both professionals and clerks were not particularly high, but the school was congenial and the city of Foxworth was a good place to live. Moreover, faculty pressures and demands weren't unreasonable. She had to agree that in his many years as Library Director Russell Barnes had built a good rapport with the people in the Administration Building, but she wondered at what price. He never really asked for anything, and she knew that if she ever got into a tangle with those people, Russell would be more concerned about protecting his image than helping her. However, nobody's perfect, she thought, and besides why worry about issues that have never arisen.

A last glance at the Landrum file revealed little else. Vicki had been highly rated in all of her performance evaluations. She was dependable and pleasant, and her attendance record was not out of line.

As Vicki entered the office, Marion could tell immediately that she was upset and nervous, and tried to put her at her ease. However, she saw quickly that Vicki had come for a reason, and until she got that off her chest she wasn't going to relax.

"How can I help you, Vicki?" Marion asked warmly. "I'm sorry to bother you like this, Ms. Rogers, but Mrs. Bogardus is on vacation and you are her superior. I thought it would be okay."

"You were perfectly right to come here, Vicki. What's the problem?"

"This morning I received my biweekly paycheck, and—here, look." Vicki proferred the check, stub and all, and Marion could see at once there was indeed a problem. The check was for $192.57, and it should have been around $300.

"Do you know what the trouble is?" Marion asked.

"Sure, it's easy to tell. Last month I signed up for the United Fund Drive, for a deduction of $2 per pay period. I know it isn't much, but it's all I can afford. You can see from the pay stub what's happened. Instead of taking out $2 for the United Fund, they're taken out $102."

"Yes, I can see that. Did you call Accounting?"

"I did. In fact, I talked to several people, including finally the university controller. I probably wouldn't normally have the nerve, but I was frightened and desperate. Ms. Rogers, I can't live and support my children for two weeks on $190." For a moment Marion thought Vicki was going to cry.

"What did they say?" Marion gently prodded.

"Oh, they saw the mistake right away. In fact they laughed about it. They said they'd take care of it on the next paycheck. Ms. Rogers, I can't wait that long."

"Didn't you ask them to issue a corrective check for the difference until the next payday?"

"Oh, sure. In fact, that's what I asked the controller when I finally talked to him. He was pleasant at first, but then he became nasty. I think it was when he found out I was just a clerk in the library. Anyway, he said doing what I asked would just be too much trouble. The payroll system is computerized, and they have to keep records for the government. He said they'd fix it in two weeks, and that's the best they could do. Ms. Rogers, you just have to help me!"

Marion felt genuine compassion, but she also felt most uneasy. She had few dealings with the people in the Administration Building, and she didn't know the controller at all. Russell took care of all that, and very well, too. And, from knowing Russell for over eight years, she had no doubt that he would not want to deal with this problem and would not appreciate her dumping it on him.

PROBLEM EXERCISE 9

"Some problems are easier than others," Frances McCardle thought after Ellen Rubin left her office. "And it's always nice when you can give an employee a positive answer." Frances was manager of the Technical Information Center of the Superior Aerospace Corp., supervising a staff of 14. Work in industry was different in many ways from her previous job as Engineering

Librarian at Eagle State University, but she felt comfortable here. What was new to her was management, and particularly management in a major corporation of more than 15,000 employees, where everything was done "by the book." The book was the manager's manual, 450 pages long. That manual covered every possible contingency, and quite a few she was sure were impossible. Frances had been issued her copy with considerable formality. The personnel manager had somberly told Frances that managers were expected to familiarize themselves with policy as contained in the manual, because employees were instructed to bring all questions to their immediate supervisor. Although supervisors in turn could refer unresolved questions to their own managers, the personnel administrator made it seem as though this manual contained everything anyone ever needed to know.

In her five months on the job she had occasion to consult the manual on a number of occasions. It had answers for every question, at least up to now.

However, for Ellen Rubin's question she didn't need to consult the manual, and she was pleased to be able to make an immediate response, particularly since the answer was what Ellen had hoped to hear. She hoped that Ellen was impressed with how quickly she had learned.

Ellen was the information center's circulation clerk. She was bright and personable, and she had been Frances' first hire three months ago. Up to now everything had worked out just fine.

What Ellen had wanted to know was whether, under company policy, she was entitled to the Jewish religious holidays of Rosh Hashannah and Yom Kippur as days off with pay. Ellen explained that she was asking for no special favors and would probably work rather than lose the money, because she had not yet worked long enough to earn vacation pay. However, the holidays were important, and if she was entitled to these days she would be very appreciative. Frances already knew the answer to her question. She rode in a car pool with George Kaplowitz, an electronics engineer at Superior Aerospace, and the group had just gotten through rearranging driving schedules because George would not be coming to work on the holidays. George had worked at Superior for over 12 years and certainly knew the policies, and he stated with conviction that it had always been company policy to grant these holidays. Frances recalled that the others in the car pool had even kidded him good-naturedly suggesting that they would hire a detective to make sure he was praying while they were slaving away.

Having answered Ellen in the affirmative, she put the matter from her mind. Ellen took both holidays as she had been told she could.

Frances was surprised when Ellen came straight into her office on the next payday, and just handled her the paycheck she had received. Ellen appeared to be too shocked to be upset, or perhaps it was just that she was confident that her manager would be able to straighten out the mistake. Superior Aerospace employees were told, over and over, that their immediate supervisors knew the rules and should be their direct contacts in all matters.

It was clear from both the paycheck and the stub that Ellen had been docked for both holidays. It was, for such a small salary, a significant amount of money. Frances reassured Ellen, and told her she would take care of the matter. She reached for the telephone to call the payroll department, but reconsidered and decided to look up the specific policy manual wording first. Frances found the appropriate policy without too much difficulty. It stated quite clearly that religious holiday pay would be given to professional employees exempt under the provision of the Fair Labor Standards Act. The policy of religious holiday pay did not apply either to clerical employees or to the hourly employees who worked on the assembly line.

PROBLEM EXERCISE 10

"She's late again," Dorothy Morgan noted grimly. "That's the fourth time this month, and something has to be done about it." Dorothy had talked to Marjorie Grimsley about her chronic lateness before, but to no discernible avail. Marjorie always had an interesting and unusual excuse, but when it came right down to it, none of them really mattered.

The Grimsleys lived in a rural area about 20 miles away from the library. One morning the electricity was off and the alarm didn't sound. On two occasions Marjorie's car wouldn't start, after her husband had already left in the second one. Once she ran into a traffic tie-up; once she had run out of gas. On one occasion she had been halfway to the library when she remembered she had forgotten her purse and decided to return for it.

All of her excuses sounded plausible, but there were just too many of them. Marjorie was one of the reference librarians at the Quantum Public Library, and she was supposed to be on duty when the library opened. After considering rotating schedules, the professional staff had voted overwhelmingly for specific weekly responsibilities. If Marjorie had preferred a later starting time, or evening work, or work on Saturday, it could probably have been worked out. Marjorie had preferred the Monday through Friday 9:00-to-5:00 schedule, because it fit in well with her husband's work schedule. The Grimsleys had no children, and liked to keep their evenings free for theaters and concerts; they also enjoyed taking weekend trips. That wasn't really any problem for the library, since there were reference librarians who preferred evenings and even weekends. Dorothy considered herself lucky in that regard, because she knew of many libraries for which scheduling caused problems and animosities.

Still, since Marjorie Grimsley had asked for the opening weekday schedule beginning at 9:00 a.m., she should be there at that time. It was true that the library wasn't really too busy that early in the morning with walk-in traffic, but that wasn't the point. The library was proud of its business reference service, and those calls sometimes did come early in the morning. Besides, if others saw Marjorie getting away with such frequent lateness, they would either resent it or decide that lateness was acceptable.

Marjorie was only a mediocre reference librarian in any case, and Dorothy Morgan felt in no mood to make further allowances. When Marjorie came in, she would undoubtedly have another innovative excuse, but Dorothy was determined to pay no attention. She would let her know that recurrence would trigger disciplinary action, and that she planned to issue a written reprimand, with copies to the chairman of the Library Board's Personnel Committee. If that didn't work either, she might ultimately have to terminate Marjorie. It would be no great loss. The Quantum Public Library, like other municipal agencies in Quantum City, had a formal and carefully spelled out disciplinary process, and a formal written reprimand was the first step. She would do it today. As director of the public library it was her responsibility.

Dorothy noticed that Marjorie wasn't the only one who was not at her desk this morning. Wilma Mellott, who staffed the genealogy and local history desk, was also late. As in Dorothy's case, Wilma could have had a later starting time, but she wanted to start at 9:00 a.m. because of her two small children. Wilma could not afford part-time work (or, as she joked, she couldn't afford a part-time salary).

The problem invariably centered around Wilma's two-year old, Kelly. A beautiful and lively youngster, Kelly also tended toward frequent if minor illnesses and emergencies, and Wilma's carefully constructed support system of nursery schools and baby-sitters sometimes came apart at the seams. At times Wilma was late, although she always came as soon as she could. Twice she hadn't made it at all. Nothing was said about docking her salary, in part because professionals weren't expected to punch a time clock, and because the entire staff was sympathetic to Wilma's predicament as a single parent of two small children. Wilma was not only cheerful and popular, she was a superb genealogy and local history librarian. Dorothy Morgan had received many glowing compliments on this service, some through the Board of Trustees.

No, Dorothy concluded, there was no similarity between the two cases. Self-indulgent Marjorie, with a lovely home, a working husband, no home pressures and lots of free time, could certainly be expected to arrange her time a little better, and to arrive as scheduled. Besides which, she was only a mediocre employee. Wilma, even if she was late as frequently, accomplished lots more after she arrived, and she was working under far greater handicaps.

Given the circumstances, Dorothy Morgan concluded, there was nothing inconsistent in reprimanding Marjorie Grimsley. Nobody could expect her also to reprimand Wilma Mellott for a situation she couldn't control.

PROBLEM EXERCISE 11

It had been a good first 10 months, Douglas Martin thought. Taking on the responsibility of directing the Millvale Public Library, with its professional staff of 60, eight branches and three bookmobiles, and at the age of 38, was no small accomplishment. The Board had been nervous about hiring him and some had openly questioned his youth and inexperience at the time of the interview. But they had hired him anyway, and Douglas supposed it was because they probably didn't have much of an alternative. Millvale was an old New England city, with the predictable mix of urban decay and high unemployment. Not the most attractive public library directorship.

Well, the Board wasn't worried any longer, he knew that, and Doug allowed himself a few moments of self-congratulations. He had captured the imagination of the Chamber of Commerce and the City Administration, had excited the community with the promise of having the best library in the state, and the local media and civic groups were solidly behind him. The library parking lot had been expanded, and money for renovating the old library building was solidly in next year's budget. He had succeeded in getting some federal and state funds, and convinced the conservative town commissioners that it was a good investment to match them rather than lose them to a city like Newton Center. He knew how to play on competition and civic pride and use them to his advantage. The budget hadn't grown much yet, but he knew it would.

Of even greater surprise and pleasure had been the reaction of the staff. He knew he wouldn't have the opportunity to make many personnel changes, and the posts that had become vacant had been filled carefully, with bright, enthusiastic, energetic and idealistic young people. He had personally gone on recruiting trips to nearby library schools, and even without a strong salary schedule he had been able to attract the people he wanted. They probably assumed that in the next few years he'd be able to do something about the salaries, too. Well, he wouldn't let them down, he promised himself that. However, even the attitudes of the carryover staff members had been a pleasant surprise. They had caught the excitement and accepted the dream. They worked willingly on committees and task forces, they contributed ideas and suggestions, and they developed innovative programs and public relations gimmicks. He had pushed his people hard, but nobody harder than himself, and he felt that they knew that and respected him. He tried to be objective and had to conclude that they also liked him. All except Hazel Hotchkiss.

It wasn't so much that Hazel disliked him. He didn't think Hazel disliked anyone. She was a charming and gracious woman, 63 years old and a direct descendent of Ebenezer Hotchkiss, who had founded Millvale over 300 years ago. Her family had always lived in Millvale, and she was a strong representative of the New England "Old Guard," the rich white Yankee Protestants who still ran the banks if not City Hall. Hazel had attended Smith and had joined the library 38 years ago, when nobody cared about library degrees. Active in every civic organization from the Music Club through the Museum League to the County Orphanage, Hazel also played bridge every Thursday evening with Mrs. Graham Whiteman. Dr. Graham Whiteman, chief of surgery of the local hospital, was the chairman of the Library Board of Trustees.

Doug Martin tried to pinpoint what bothered him about Hazel. There were certainly no problems at the West Side branch, which Hazel had directed (presided over was probably a better description) for the last 25 years. The west side of Millvale was the "right side of the tracks," where the old money and much of the new wealth lived. The older users of the library were people very much like Hazel, and they felt comfortable with her. However, even the children liked and appreciated her regal but kind bearing, and the younger staff members seemed to adore her.

What then bothered him about Hazel? Undoubtedly, it was the fact that although she never confronted or opposed him on any issue, she managed to ignore him quite successfully. It was as though all of the changes and innovations were totally irrelevant to her. She had no objection to his doing whatever it was he did, but it had nothing to do with her or the West Side Branch. He tried to remember the last department head meeting she had attended, and couldn't recall. She never unreasonably refused to come, she just always had a good excuse. None of the policy changes and instructions issued for the entire system had ever been implemented at West, and if other staff members noticed at all they never commented. Hazel Hotchkiss simply lived in a library world of her own, without needing anyone.

She accepted her monthly salary, but Doug suspected she did it only to be gracious and to avoid causing embarrassment. She certainly didn't need the money. She already had bought and paid for her retirement condominium in Florida, to which she would be moving, she had announced to Mrs. Whiteman and he had heard from Dr. Whiteman, when she reached the age of 65. Millvale no longer had a mandatory retirement policy, but Hazel Hotchkiss had apparently decided for herself that this was a proper time to retire. She had never informed Doug—in fact she never informed him of anything. On the two occasions on which he had visited her library she had received him as courteously and graciously as she instinctively did everything, and then shown him through HER library. He could really find nothing wrong, except for the obvious fact that what happened at West had nothing to do with overall Millvale library policy. During those visits he felt like an outsider, almost like a little boy. She called him Mr. Martin, and so he called her Miss Hotchkiss, although he was on a first-name basis with everyone else in the library and with the mayor. He didn't imagine anyone had called her Hazel to her face except her mother.

In any case, the situation with Hazel Hotchkiss annoyed and disturbed him, even though he couldn't quite decide where the main problem was. Doug was a proud and self-confident young man, and it bothered him to realize that Hazel Hotchkiss was on his mind, while at the same time he was sure she never gave him a second thought.

PROBLEM EXERCISE 12

As soon as she heard about it, Gwen Peters knew that the municipal auditorium speech by CIA Director Parsons would cause some polarization in the community. The CIA was consistently unpopular with some people in the community, but its activities were just as staunchly defended by others.

She knew where the sympathies of Mayor Callahan lay. After all, it was he who had been instrumental in the invitation to Parsons. When it was first announced two months ago, Gwen assumed it was part of Mayor Callahan's plan to secure the backing from the right wing of his own political party, as he began his primary campaign for the vacant Senate seat.

Gwen considered herself a political moderate, and not at all committed to any party or point of view. She dealt with each issue and candidacy as it arose, and felt quite comfortably not only that such an intellectually evenhanded approach showed reason and balance, but that it was appropriate for anyone who as director of the public library had to meet with civic groups of various persuasions. It was better not to be stereotyped, and she felt that in no way did this compromise her right to vote or express her convictions, when she did decide.

Whatever his political views, Mayor Callahan had caused no problems for the library. Although it shared the financial concerns of any member of a major urban community, the library had not fared any worse than other municipal agencies, and had certainly done better than some public libraries about which she read in professional journals. Furthermore, although the community certainly had its share of demogogues who would censor individual thought if they had the chance (demogogues came, Gwen knew, from both the right and the left), there had been no problems here. Mayor Callahan ruled firmly, and he brooked no such nonsense in his close alliance with the community's business leaders. Gwen wasn't sure about his own commitment to open access to information, but censorship was bad publicity and certainly bad for the aspirations of a potential senator.

In any case, the invitation to CIA director Parsons to speak at the municipal auditorium Saturday evening had caused little stir at the time, and would probably not have caused much attention even now, except for the happenings in South America during the last two weeks. A leftist government had been bloodily overthrown, and the evidence was confusing and contradictory. Gwen wasn't sure what had happened, and she didn't really believe anyone could be sure. Of course that didn't stop the firebrands of either the right or left, who always seemed to have conclusions which required no facts to support them.

Gwen knew that not everyone on the library staff felt as she did, and it appeared to her that there was more sentiment for the left than for the right. Probably the most outspoken of the staff was Warren Martin. A student activist who chose to become a librarian, Warren was involved in every protest movement she could think of. However, he was never blatant or offensive on the job, and he was a good reference librarian.

The library would be closed on Saturday evening, and even if there were protesters and hecklers, as it was surmised there might be, it had nothing to do with the library or with her. She had no intention of attending either the talk or the demonstration. She did decide to watch the 11:00 news, though, and found that there had indeed been some trouble, although fortunately no arrests or injuries. Tomatoes and eggs had been thrown at Parsons as he arrived, and protesters marched prominently in front of the auditorium.

She was not surprised to see Warren Martin among the protesters. She could identify him clearly in the TV lights. She was surprised, though, at the sign he was carrying, which said, "Keep Your Murdering Hands Off Latin America." On the same large sign, in letters equally large, it also said "Employees of the Public Library." Gwen saw no other library employees except Warren, although she couldn't be sure. She did wonder about his right to carry such a sign, free speech notwithstanding.

In any case, she was fairly certain that if the mayor or any of his aides had noticed this (and how could they miss it?), she would be hearing about the matter Monday morning, if not sooner.

Selected Bibliography

LIBRARY MONOGRAPHS

Allerton Park Institute. *Supervision of Employees in Libraries.* Edited by R. E. Stevens. Champaign, IL: University of Illinois, 1979.

Anderson, A. J. *Problems in Library Management.* Littleton, CO: Libraries Unlimited, 1981.

Association of Research Libraries. *Changing Role of the ARL Library Personnel Officer.* Washington, DC: ARL Systems and Procedures Exchange Center, 1978.

Association of Research Libraries. *Performance Appraisal in ARL Libraries.* Washington, DC: ARL Systems and Procedures Exchange Center, 1979.

Bommer, M. R. W., and Chorba, R. W. *Decision Making for Library Management.* White Plains, NY: Knowledge Industry Publications, Inc., 1982.

Booz, Allen, and Hamilton, Inc. *Organization and Staffing of the Libraries of Columbia University,* sponsored by a grant from the Council on Library Resources. Westport, CT: Redgrave Information Resources Corp., 1973.

Buckland, Michael K. "The Management of Libraries and Information Centers." In *Annual Review of Information Science and Technology,* vol. 9. Washington, DC: American Society for Information Science, 1974.

Cowley, John. *Personnel Management in Libraries.* Hamden, CT: Bingley, 1982.

Creth, Sheila. "Personnel Planning, Job Analysis, and Job Evaluation, with Special Reference to Academic Libraries." In *Advances in Librarianship,* vol. 12. New York: Academic Press, 1982.

Creth, Sheila, and Duda, F., eds. *Personnel Administration in Libraries.* New York: Neal-Schuman Publishers, 1981.

Dougherty, Richard M., et. al. *Scientific Management of Library Operations.* 2nd ed. Metuchen, NJ: Scarecrow Press, 1982.

Evans, G. E. *Management Techniques for Librarians.* New York: Academic Press, 1976.

Foster, D. L. *Managing the Catalog Department.* 2nd ed. Metuchen, NJ: Scarecrow Press, 1982.

Herbert, Clara W. *Personnel Administration in Public Libraries.* Chicago: American Library Association, 1939.

Johnson, E. R., and Mann, S. H. *Organization Development for Academic Libraries: An Evaluation of the Management Review and Analysis Program.* Westport, CT: Greenwood Press, 1980.

Lee, Sul H., ed. *Emerging Trends in Library Organization: What Influences Change.* Ann Arbor, MI: Pierian Press, 1978.

Lowell, Mildred H. *The Management of Libraries and Information Centers.* 4 volumes. Metuchen, NJ: Scarecrow Press, 1971.

Maloney, R. K. M., ed. *Personnel Development in Libraries: Proceedings of the 13th Annual Symposium,* sponsored by the alumni and the faculty of the Rutgers University Graduate School of Library Service, 1977.

Marchant, Maurice P. *Participative Management in Academic Libraries.* Westport, CT: Greenwood Press, 1976.

Martin, Murray S. *Issues in Personnel Management in Academic Libraries.* Greenwich, CT: JAI Press, 1981.

McClure, C. R., and Samuels, A. R., eds. *Strategies for Library Administration: Concepts and Approaches.* Littleton, CO: Libraries Unlimited, 1982.

Personnel Evaluation Institute, Eastern Illinois University. *Proceedings of the Personnel Evaluation Institute,* held at Charleston, IL, October 24–26, 1976. Edited by F. M. Pollard. Eastern Illinois University Dept. of Library Science, 1976.

Reeves, W. J. *Librarians as Professionals: The Occupation's Impact on Library Work Arrangements.* Lexington, MA: D. C. Heath & Co., 1980.

Ricking, Myrl, and Booth, Robert E. *Personnel Utilization in Libraries: A Systems Approach.* Chicago: American Library Association, 1974.

Rizzo, J. R. *Management for Librarians: Fundamentals and Issues.* Westport, CT: Greenwood Press, 1980.

Sager, Donald J. *Managing the Public Library.* White Plains, NY: Knowledge Industry Publications, Inc., 1984.

Shaffer, Kenneth R. *Twenty-five Short Cases in Library Personnel Administration.* Hamden, CT: Shoe String Press, 1959.

Shuman, Bruce A. *The River Bend Case Book: Problems in Public Library Service.* Phoenix, AZ: Oryx Press, 1981.

Stebbins, K. B. *Personnel Administration in Libraries.* 2nd ed. Metuchen, NJ: Scarecrow Press, 1966.

Stueart, R. D., and Eastlick, J. T. *Library Management*. 2nd ed. Littleton, CO: Libraries Unlimited, 1981.

Sullivan, Peggy, and Ptacek, William. *Public Libraries: Smart Practices in Personnel.* Littleton, CO: Libraries Unlimited, 1982.

Wasserman, Paul, and Bundy, Mary Lee. *Reader in Library Administration.* Washington, DC: Microcard Editions, 1968.

White, Herbert S. *Automation: Where and When to Begin.* Conference Proceedings of the Special Libraries Association, Washington, DC: Chapter Documentation Group, 1966.

White, Herbert S. *Managing the Special Library.* White Plains, NY: Knowledge Industry Publications, Inc., 1984.

LIBRARY PERIODICAL ARTICLES

Bailey, Martha J. "Requirements for Middle Managerial Positions." *Special Libraries* 69 (September 1978):323–331.

Conroy, B. "Human Element: Staff Development in the Electronic Library." *Drexel Library Quarterly* 17 (Fall 1981):91–106.

Creth, Sheila. "Conducting an Effective Employment Interview." *Journal of Academic Librarianship* 4 (November 1978):356–360.

DeFichy, Wendy. "Affirmative Action: Equal Opportunity for Women in Library Management." *College and Research Libraries* 34 (May 1973):195–201.

DeGennaro, Richard. "Library Administration and New Management Systems." *Library Journal* 103 (December 15, 1978): 2477–2482.

DeGennaro, Richard. "Theory vs. Practice in Library Management." *Library Journal* 108 (July 1983):1818-1821.

DeProspo, Ernest R. "Personnel Evaluation as an Impetus to Growth." *Library Trends* 20 (July 1971):60-70.

Dickinson, D. W. "Some Reflections on Participative Management in Libraries." *College and Research Libraries* 39 (July 1978): 253-262.

Donahue, M. "Personnel Administration in the Academic Library." Specialist in Librarianship thesis, University of Wisconsin-Madison, 1971.

Dougherty, Richard M. "Role of Management Consultants in the 1980s." *Library Trends* 28 (Winter 1980):425-436.

Dragon, Andrea C. "Self-description and Subordinate Descriptions of Leader Behavior of Library Administrators." Ph.D. thesis, University of Minnesota, 1977.

Drucker, Peter F. "Managing the Public Service Institution." *College and Research Libraries* 37 (January 1976):4-14.

Duda, F. "Columbia's Two-track System of Professional Ranks and Position Categories." *College and Research Libraries* 4 (July 1980):295-304.

Dutton, B. G. "Job Assessment and Job Evaluation." *ASLIB Proceedings* 28 (April 1976):144-160.

Eggleton, R. B. "Academic Libraries, Participative Management and Risky Shift." *Journal of Academic Librarianship* 5 (November 1979):270-273.

Epstein, Susan Baerg. "Implementation of an Automated System." *Library Journal* 108 (September 15, 1983):1771-1772.

Gore, Daniel. "Things Your Boss Never Told You About Library Management." *Library Journal* 102 (April 1, 1977):765-770.

Harrington, J. "Human Relations in Management During Periods of Economic Uncertainty." *Drexel Library Quarterly* 17 (Spring 1981):16-26.

Heim, Kathleen M. "Toward a Work-force Analysis of the School Library Media Professional." *School Media Quarterly* 9 (Summer 1981):235-249.

Hilton, R. C. "Performing Evaluation of Library Personnel." *Special Libraries* 69 (November 1978):429-434.

Hodge, S. P. "Performance Appraisals: Developing a Sound Legal and Managerial System." *College and Research Libraries* 44 (July 1983):235-244.

Howard, Edward N. "The Orbital Organization." *Library Journal* 95 (May 1, 1970):1712-1715.

Jackson, Ruth L. M. "Organization and Development of Selected Personnel Management Functions in the Field of American Librarianship 1876-1969." Ph.D. thesis, Indiana University, 1976.

Johnson, M. "Performance Appraisal of Librarians: A Survey." *College and Research Libraries* 33 (September 1972):359-367.

Kroll, H. R. "Beyond Evaluation: Performance Appraisal as a Planning and Motivational Tool in Libraries." *Journal of Academic Librarianship* 9 (March 1983):27-32.

Lewis, M. "Management by Objective: Review, Application and Relationship with Job Satisfaction and Performance." *Journal of Academic Librarianship* 5 (January 1980):329-334.

Luquire, Wilson. "Attitudes Toward Automation/Innovation in Academic Libraries." *Journal of Academic Librarianship* 8 (January 1983):344-351.

Lynch, Beverly P. "Libraries as Bureaucracies." *Library Trends* 27 (Winter 1979):259-267.

Mahmoodi, Susan H. "Identification of Competencies of Librarians in Public Service Areas of Public Libraries." Ph.D. thesis, University of Minnesota, 1978.

Mason, Ellsworth. "The Great Gas Bubble Prick't"; or "Computers Revealed—by a Gentleman of Quality." *College and Research Libraries* 32 (May 1971):183-196. Reactions to article. *College and Research Libraries* 32 (September 1971):384-392.

Munn, Robert F. "The Bottomless Pit, or the Academic Library as Viewed from the Administration Building." *College and Research Libraries* 29 (January 1968):51-54.

Mussman, K. "Socio-technical Theory and Job Design in Libraries." *College and Research Libraries* 39 (January 1978):20-28.

Plate, Kenneth H., and Stone, Elizabeth W. "Factors Affecting Librarians' Job Satisfaction." *Library Quarterly* 44 (April 1974): 97-110.

Shaughnessy, Thomas W. "Library Administration in Support of Emerging Service Patterns." *Library Trends* 28 (Fall 1979): 139-149.

Shaughnessy, Thomas W. "Technology and the Structure of Libraries." *Libri* 32 (June 1982):149-155.

Stead, B. A., and Scammel, R. W. "Study of the Relationship of Role Conflict, the Need for Role Clarity, and Job Satisfaction for Professional Librarians." *Library Quarterly* 50 (July 1980): 310-323.

Stuart-Stubbs, Basil. "Levels of Incompetence: The Peter Principle Applied to Libraries." *IPLO Quarterly* 12 (October 1970):43-56.

Swanson, R. W. "Organization Theory Related to Library Management." *Canadian Library Journal* 30 (July 1973):356–364.

Weber, David C., and Kess, T. "Comparable Rewards: The Case for Equal Compensation for Non-administrative Expertise." *Library Journal* 103 (April 15, 1978):824–827.

White, Herbert S. "Cost-effectiveness and Cost-benefit Determinations in Special Libraries." *Special Libraries* 70 (April 1979): 163–169.

White, Herbert S. "Library Management in the Tight Budget Seventies: Problems, Challenges, and Opportunities." *Medical Library Association Bulletin* 65 (January 1977): 6–12.

White, Herbert S. "Management: A Strategy for Change." *Canadian Library Journal* 35 (October 1978):329–339.

White, Herbert S. "Subverted by Pragmatism." *Library Journal* 109 (May 1, 1984):861–862.

White, Herbert S., and Paris, Marion. "Employer Preferences and the Library Education Curriculum." The *Library Quarterly* 55 (January 1985):1–33.

Willard, D. D. "Seven Realities of Library Administration." *Library Journal* 101 (January 15, 1976):311–317.

GENERAL MANAGEMENT MONOGRAPHS

Adams, Sexton. *Modern Personnel Management.* Houston, TX: Gulf Publishing Co., 1981.

Appley, Lawrence A. *The Human Element in Personnel Management and the Responsibilities of the Administrator.* Washington, DC: Society for Personnel Administration, 1941.

Argyris, Chris. *Integrating the Individual and the Organization.* New York: John Wiley & Sons, 1964.

Beach, Dale S. *Personnel: The Management of People at Work.* 4th ed. New York: Macmillan Publishing, 1980.

Belker, Loren B. *The First-time Manager: A Practical Guide to the Management of People.* New York: AMACOM, 1978.

Benton, Lewis R. *Supervision and Management.* New York: McGraw-Hill, 1972.

Berenson, Conrad. *Job Descriptions: How to Write and Use Them.* Revised ed. Santa Monica, CA: Personnel Journal, 1976.

Brown, James D. *The Human Nature of Organizations.* New York: AMACOM, 1973.

Chruden, Herbert J., and Sherman, Arthur W. *Personnel Management.* Cincinnati, OH: Southwest Publishing Co., 1976.

Cowan, John. *The Self-reliant Manager.* New York: AMACOM, 1977.

Dooher, M. Joseph, and Marquis, Vivienne, eds. *The Supervisor's Management Guide, for All Who Supervise Others.* New York: AMACOM, 1949.

Drucker, Peter F. *Technology, Management, and Society.* New York: Harper & Row, 1973.

Flippo, Edwin B. *Personnel Management.* 5th ed. New York: McGraw-Hill, 1980.

French, Wendell L. *The Personnel Management Process: Human Resources Administration and Development.* 4th ed. Boston: Houghton Mifflin, 1978.

Fulmer, Robert M., and Franklin, Stephen G. *Supervision: Principles of Professional Management.* 2nd ed. New York: Macmillan Publishing, 1982.

Herzberg, Frederick. *Work and the Nature of Man.* Cleveland, OH: World Publishing Co., 1966.

Hunsaker, Phillip L. *The Art of Managing People.* Englewood Cliffs, NJ: Prentice-Hall, 1980.

Irish, Richard K. *If Things Don't Improve Soon I May Ask You to Fire Me.* Garden City, NY: Anchor Press, 1975.

Johnson, Robert G. *The Appraisal Interview Guide.* New York: AMACOM, 1979.

Jucius, Michael J. *Personnel Management.* 9th ed. Homewood, IL: R. D. Irwin, 1979.

Killian, Ray A. *Managers Must Lead!* Revised ed. New York: AMACOM, 1979.

Kirkpatrick, Donald L. *How to Improve Performance Through Appraisal and Coaching.* New York: AMACOM, 1982.

Laird, Donald A. *The Psychology of Selecting Employees.* 3rd ed. New York: McGraw-Hill, 1937.

Laird, Donald A., and Laird, Eleanor C. *The Technique of Delegation.* New York: McGraw-Hill, 1957.

Lindo, David K. *Supervision Can Be Easy.* New York: AMACOM, 1979.

Maslow, Abraham. *Motivation and Personality.* New York: Harper & Row, 1954.

McGregor, Douglas. *The Human Side of Enterprise.* New York: McGraw-Hill, 1960.

Mindell, Mark G. *Employee Values in a Changing Society.* New York: AMACOM, 1981.

Novit, Mitchell S. *Essentials of Personnel Management.* Englewood Cliffs, NJ: Prentice-Hall, 1979.

Odiorne, George S. *Personnel Administration by Objectives.* Homewood, IL: R. D. Irwin, 1971.

Odiorne, George S. *Training by Objectives: An Economic Approach to Management Training.* New York: Macmillan Publishing, 1970.

Ouchi, William. *Theory Z: How American Business Can Meet the Japanese Challenge.* Reading, MA: Addison-Wesley, 1981.

Parkinson, C. Northcote. *Parkinson's Law and Other Studies in Administration.* Boston: Houghton-Mifflin, 1957.

Pell, Arthur R. *Recruiting, Training, and Motivating Volunteer Workers.* New York: Pilot Books, 1972.

Peter, Laurence J. *The Peter Principle.* New York: William Morrow, 1969.

Pigors, Paul J. *Personnel Administration: A Point of View and a Method.* 9th ed. New York: McGraw-Hill, 1981.

Randsdall, William K. *Clerical Job Evaluations.* Cleveland, OH: Association for Systems Management, 1979.

Roseman, Edward. *Managing Employee Turnover: A Positive Approach.* New York: AMACOM, 1981.

Roseman, Edward. *Managing the Problem Employee.* New York: AMACOM, 1982.

Sayall, Henri. *Work and People: An Economic Evaluation of Job Enrichment.* New York: Oxford Press, 1981.

Steinmetz, Lawrence L. *The Art and Skill of Delegation.* Reading, MA: Addison-Wesley, 1976.

Valentine, Raymond F. *Initiative and Managerial Power.* New York: AMACOM, 1973.

Van Maanen, John, and Schein, Edgar H. "Career Development." In *Improving Life at Work,* edited by J. Richard Hackman and J. Lloyd Suttle. Santa Monica, CA: Goodyear Publishing Co., 1977.

Wasmath, William J., and Greenhalgh, Leonard. *Effective Supervision: Developing Your Skills Through Critical Incidents.* Englewood Cliffs, NJ: Prentice-Hall, 1979.

GENERAL MANAGEMENT PERIODICALS

Baird, L. S., and Beccia, P. J. "Potential Misuse of Overtime." *Personnel Psychology* 33 (Autumn 1980):557–565.

Baker, H. K., and Holmberg, S. R. "Stepping Up to Supervision: Being Popular Isn't Enough." *Supervisory Management* 27 (January 1982):12–18.

Bartolome, F., and Evans, P. A. L. "Must Success Cost So Much?" *Harvard Business Review* 58 (March/April 1980):137–148.

Caruth, D. "How to Communicate to Be Understood." *Supervisory Management* 27 (February 1982):30–37.

Dodd, W. E., and Pesci, M. L. "Managing Morale Through Survey Feedback." *Business Horizons* 20 (June 1977):36–45.

Feldman, D. C. "Socialization Process that Helps New Recruits Succeed." *Personnel* 57 (March 1980):11–23.

Flynn, W. R., and Stratton, W. E. "Managing Problem Employees." *Human Resources Management* 20 (Summer 1981):28–32.

Franklin, W. H. "Why You Can't Motivate Everyone." *Supervisory Management* 25 (April 1980):21–28.

Gilmore, C. B., and Fannin, W. R. "Dual Career Couple: A Challenge to Personnel in the Eighties." *Business Horizons* 25 (May/June 1982):36–41.

Grant, P. C. "Why Employee Motivation Has Declined in America." *Personnel Journal* 61 (December 1982):905-909.

Greller, M. M. "Nature of Subordinate Participation in the Appraisal Interview." *Academic Management Journal* 21 (December 1978):646-658.

Hedberg, Bo, et al. "Camping on Seesaws. Prescriptions for a Self-Designing Organization." *Administrative Sciences Quarterly* 21(1) (1976):41-65.

Hodge, J. "Common-sensical Approach to Supervising Minorities." *Supervisory Management* 28 (September 1983):24-27.

Hollingsworth, A. T., and Al-Jafary, A. R. A. "Why Supervisors Don't Delegate and Employees Won't Accept Responsibility." *Supervisory Management* 28 (April 1983):12-17.

Hunsaker, J. S. "Work and Family Life Must Be Integrated." *Personnel Administration* 28 (April 1983):87-91.

Ivancevich, J. M. "Different Goal Setting Treatments and Their Effects on Performance and Job Satisfaction." *Academic Management Journal* 20 (September 1977):406-419.

Kikoski, J. F., and Litterer, J. A. "Effective Communication in the Performance Appraisal Interview." *Public Personnel Management* 12 (Spring 1983):33-42.

Klinger, D. E. "Changing Role of Personnel Management in the 1980s." *Personnel Administration* 24 (September 1979): 41-48.

Kovach, K. A. "Why Motivational Theories Don't Work." *SAM Advanced Management Journal* 45 (Spring 1980):54-59.

Kushell, R. E. "How to Reduce Turnover by Creating a Positive Work Climate." *Personnel Journal* 58 (August 1979):551-555.

Matthieson, E. and Hollwitz, J. "Giving Instructions That Get Followed." *Supervisory Management* 28 (May 1983):20-24.

Odiorne, G. S. "Personnel Management for the '80s." *Personnel Administration* 22 (August 1977):20-24.

O'Reilly, C. A., and Weitz, B. A. "Managing Marginal Employees: The Use of Warnings and Dismissals." *Administrative Science Quarterly* 25 (September 1980):467-484.

Patten, T. H., Jr. "Job Evaluation and Job Enlargement: A Collision Course?" *Human Resource Management* 16 (Winter 1977): 2-8.

Rosenbaum, B. L. "Understanding and Using Motivation." *Supervisory Management* 24 (January 1979):9-13.

Schuler, R. S. "Effective Use of Communication to Minimize Employee Stress." *Personnel Administration* 24 (June 1979): 40-44.

Stanton, E. S. "A Critical Reevaluation of Motivation, Management, and Productivity." *Personnel Journal* 62 (March 1983): 208-214.

Steele, Lowell. "Managers' Misconceptions About Technology." *Harvard Business Review* 61 (November/December 1983): 133-140.

White, R. N. "Documenting Employee Problems." *Supervisory Management* 27 (August 1982):38-42.

Index

Abdication, 65, 81
Accountability, 92
Administrative management, 10
Affirmative action, 106–107, 109
Alienation, 55
Ambition, 16
Authority, 14, 92–93
  sources of, 75–77
Automation, 34–35
  and decision making, 65
  and job security, 60–61
  objections to, 62–63
  planning, 58–60, 63–64
  reasons for, 66–67
  and recalcitrants, 68–69

Behavioral scientists, 11–12, 124
Booz, Allen, & Hamilton, Inc., 30
Branch libraries, 25
Budgets, libraries, 1–2
Bureaucratic model, 10–11

Career stages, 114
Change, fear of, 15, 62
Charisma, 77–78
Classical theories, 10–11
Client, organization by, 26
Columbia University Libraries, 30–31

Communication, 16–17, 152–159
Competence, 76
Consultative management, 84, 87–89, 90, 94, 151
Continuing education, 118–121
Courage, 20–21

Decision making, 31, 78
  avoidance, 79–82
  and communication, 150–151
  orbital, 90–91
  styles, 83–84
  See also Consultative management; Participatory management
Decline, management of, 43–44
Delegation, 20, 91–95
Disciplinary action, 135–138
Drucker, Peter, 57, 58, 64, 65, 159

Education, 114–116, 117–121, 168
Egalitarian salary systems, 139–141
Epstein, Susan Baerg, 63
Equal opportunity employment, 106–107

Evaluation
  of candidates, 102–106
  performance, 130–132

Faculty status, 6, 89
Fairness, 14–15, 50–51
Firing, 138
Flexible scheduling, 12
Functions, organization by, 24–25

Goals, 5, 39, 52
  See also Objectives
Grievances, 37

Halo effect, 105–106
Hedberg, Bo, 43–44
Herzberg, Frederick, 124
Humanists (librarians), 4–5

Interviewing (candidates), 104–106

Japanese model, 45–47
Job descriptions, 128–129
Job design, 123–128
Job ratings, 143–145
Job security, 53–54, 60–61

Leadership, 18–19, 72–73
  traits, 74–75
Letters of recommendation, 102
Line management, 27
  and staff employees, 33–34
Loyalty, 21
Luquire, Wilson, 61

Management Review and Analysis Program (MRAP), 158
Maslow, Abraham, 48, 51–52, 61
Medical Library Association, 120
Meetings, 153–154
Merit salary systems, 141–142
Motivation, 40, 53–54
  for continuing education, 120
  and objectives, 42
  theories of, 9
Munn, Robert, 39

Needs, hierarchy of, 48–50, 51–52

Objectives, 7, 41–42
  Japanese model, 45–47
  management by, 41
  and motivation, 42
  staff involvement, 44–45, 52–53
  unfulfilled, 42–43, 55
OCLC, 59
Open-mindedness, 16
Oral communication, 152–154
Orbital decision making, 90–91
Organic systems, 29–31
Organizational structures, types of, 24–26
Ouchi, William, 113
Overqualified employees, 98–100

Participatory management, 17, 54, 84, 86–87, 88, 89–90, 94
Paternalism, 45, 169
Performance evaluation, 130–132
Personnel departments, 32, 33, 35–37
Peter, Laurence, 72, 74
Planning for automation, 58–60, 63–64
Priorities, establishing, 5, 19–20
Programmers, 34
Projects, 27
Promotions, 54, 72, 100–101, 132–134

Referent power, 76
Responsibility, 14, 92–93
Resumes, 103–104

Salaries, 1–2, 36, 49, 107
   criteria for determining, 142–143
   egalitarian systems, 139–141
   merit systems, 141–142
   ranges, 145–146
Scientific management, 10, 57, 123

Seniority system, 53, 140
Staff functions, 27–28, 31–33
   "assistants to," 32
   personnel departments, 32, 33, 35–37
   systems, 34–35
Steele, Lowell, 66, 67
Strikes, 164–165
Suspensions, 138
Systems analysts, 34
Systems approach, 58

Taylor, Frederick, 9, 10, 51, 57, 123
Testing (for jobs), 107–108
Theory Z, 113
Training, 60, 115, 116–118, 168
Transfers, 134–135

Unions, 13, 35, 163–165
   and egalitarianism, 140
   history, 161–163

Vertical communication, 156–159

Weber, Max, 10–11
Written communication, 155–156

ABOUT THE AUTHOR

Herbert S. White is dean of the School of Library and Information Science, Indiana University. He was previously senior vice president, Institute for Scientific Information; executive director, NASA Scientific and Technical Information Facility; and program manager, IBM Corporate Technical Information Center.

White is former president of both the Special Libraries Association and the American Society for Information Science; treasurer and member of the executive committee, International Federation for Documentation; director, American Federation of Information Processing Societies; chairman, Governmental Relations Committee, Association of American Library Schools; and member, American Library Association Committee on Accreditation.

Widely known as a writer, speaker and consultant, he is the author of *Publishers and Libraries—A Study of Scholarly and Research Journals* (with Bernard M. Fry, 1976), *Managing the Special Library: Strategies for Success within the Larger Organization* (Knowledge Industry Publications, Inc., 1984) and more than 50 articles and book chapters. He won the 1976 ASIS award for Information Science Book of the Year and has won numerous other awards for research papers.

White holds a B.S. in chemistry from the College of the City of New York and an M.L.S. from Syracuse University.